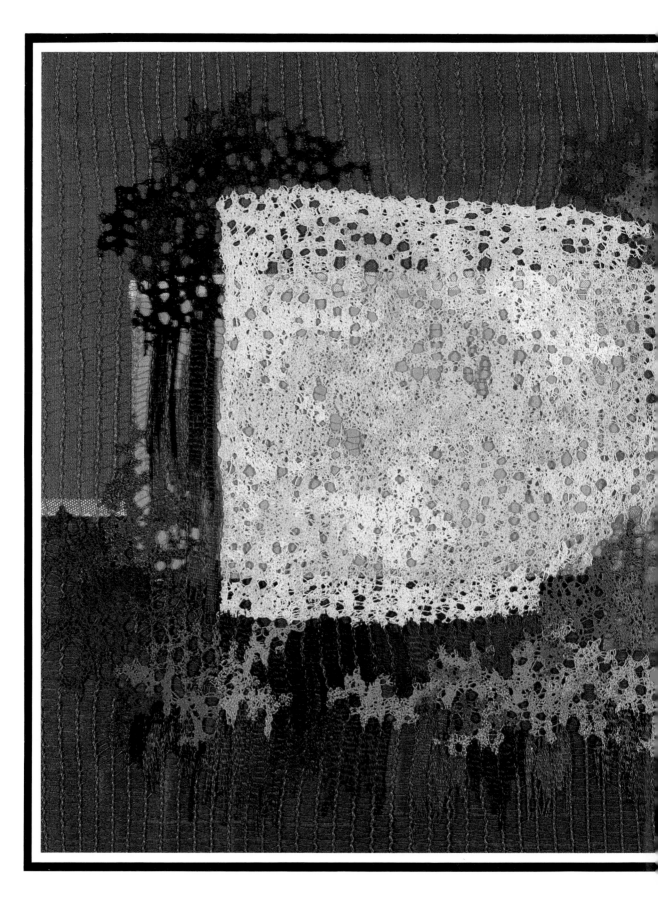

JOY CLUCAS

The New Machine Embroidery

A DAVID & CHARLES CRAFT BOOK

Half-title
*Feather and presser foot satin stitches, 25.5×15cm (10×
15in). Notice the soft ends of the presser foot stems; the frame
is pushed to open out the stitches. The looped texture of the
straight feather stitch lines must be closely worked to have any
effect.*

Title page
*'Breakthrough' by Joy Clucas. This piece is worked on a plastic
vegetable bag picked up on market day. It is worked entirely
in free straight stitching. As it is an open fabric, both threads
can be seen, giving great richness of colour.*

Author's work photographed by Geoff Meadowcroft

British Library Cataloguing in Publication Data

Clucas, Joy
   The new machine embroidery.
   1. Embroidery, Machine
   I. Title
   746.44'028   TS1783

   ISBN 0–7153–8999–8

Typeset by ABM Typographics Limited, Hull
Printed in West Germany
by Mohndruck GmbH
for David & Charles Publishers plc
Brunel House   Newton Abbot   Devon

Distribution in the United States by
Sterling Publishing Co, Inc
2 Park Avenue, New York, NY 10016

CONTENTS

Introduction

There have been many recent changes in both sewing machines and materials. Sewing machines have been computerised, involving changes in the way they are operated, and the choice of machines is now bewildering. The machine embroiderer has special needs, and these are not always catered for. Because it is not possible to get the best features of every machine in one, I have given a comprehensive list of guidelines for prospective buyers.

The choice of fabrics, threads and sewable non-woven materials is always increasing, giving rise to inventive techniques in all textile disciplines. One of the most exciting new developments is the use of a water soluble plastic, which makes fine lacework much easier than earlier methods.

During my travels in Australia, New Zealand, America and Canada I have met many wonderful people to whom I owe thanks for the ideas they have shared with me, which have contributed to making this a more informative book. I will not say 'complete' because I do not believe there is any end to the creative potential of the machine.

I started machine embroidery at art school in 1950. I clearly remember that for the first month I did not succeed in doing anything. It would have been encouraging to my students today had I kept my early efforts, but you never envisage the day that you might teach someone else. Then I had a major breakthrough, my teacher looked at me with astonishment and said: 'Joy, you have actually done something.' So take heart, those of you who find it difficult; the skill will come.

The machines in college were heavy trade embroidery machines that had no presser foot, and only did straight stitch, eyelets, and satin stitch shaped with a knee control. When I left college three years later I was thrown on the resources of the domestic machine, and set about exploiting it.

Most of the variations in this book have been dis-

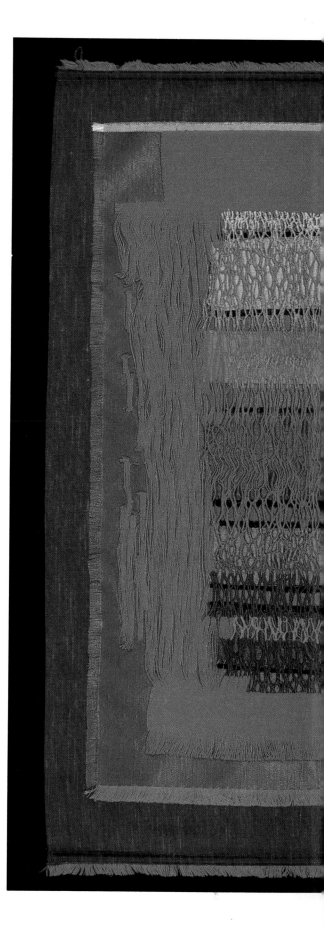

'Net Result' by Joy Clucas, 59×77cm (23½× 30½in). The colour order was planned first, then alternate bands were pulled and stitched. The loose fabric threads were cut and stitched at frequent intervals with running zigzag and the presser foot.

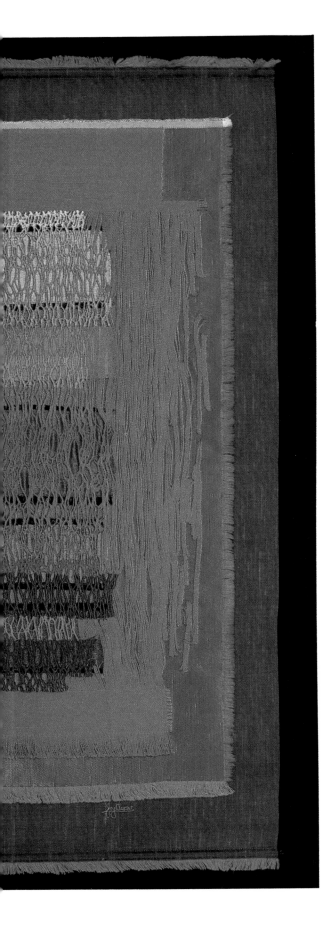

covered by trial and error, as you would do if you had unlimited time. All that I have discovered is summarised here. The book may seem rather technical at first glance. It has to be, but it is all very logical. I have done my best to make things clear by giving reasons when necessary. For those of you familiar with my first book, do not think because you see all the stitches listed that it is merely an updated version. In fact, there is a great deal of new information about methods and materials; the stitch samples also are extremely varied. They are motifs that could be adapted in a dozen different ways for your own purposes. It is a 'how to do it' book and, because there are not too many books on the subject already, it has been necessary to cover the basics; even so I think the reader will find some useful tips.

Although there are many books on design this can still be a stumbling block. I hope that both the text and the illustrations in this book show which techniques will mix well and how to develop a source of design.

Machine embroidery is one of the richest of crafts. Because colour is so important, I thought it worthwhile to use three colour plates for groups of the stitch samples. Most of them are my own, for which I make no apology, as they best express what I am trying to convey. The work of several others is included; I have chosen those designs because they delight me, as I hope they will you, and because they are very different from anything I might do.

This book covers many variations of stitches and appliqué, with numerous design ideas; in short it is a comprehensive guide for those who use their machines creatively.

'Owl' by Stephen Ballard, age 9, Bishop William Ward School, Colchester, 26.5×20cm (10½×7¾in). Children have an instinctive feeling for design; he has achieved something that adults find difficult — the balancing of diagonals.

The Cost of Machines

The most sophisticated machines on the market today cost more than the most expensive items of domestic equipment, such as washing machines and freezers. It is important, therefore, to research thoroughly the subject before you buy one. There is a vast range to choose from, both in price and quality. The criterion 'that you get what you pay for' is probably more true of sewing machines than of anything else. However, if you can afford the considerable outlay, a really good sewing machine, even though in constant use, but properly cared for, should last a lifetime. A poor quality machine, which constantly breaks threads or misses stitches, is so discouraging to a beginner that she may be put off for life. If you cannot afford the best machine, it is worth considering a good secondhand one. Unless you know a lot about machines, it is wise to buy one with a guarantee from a reputable dealer. Many women buy machines, find that they do not use them and sell them, thus there are bargains to be had. By the same token you must be sure that you will use fully the one you buy.

Machine embroidery is a craft that must be experienced to discover how varied and creative it can be. You must also assess what aspects of the craft interest you most. It is an expensive experiment buying a machine to find out. If you cannot attend a class, try to discuss the subject with someone who machine embroiders, and read all the books you can find.

Machine embroidery is not new. Not long after the invention of the sewing machine its decorative potential was realised. Elaborate, beautiful lace work, involving considerable skill, was executed on treadle machines before the turn of the century. Satin stitch was worked by moving the hoop from side to side with each stitch, necessitating perfect co-ordination of foot and hand. The advent of the swing needle machine (not to mention the use of electricity) made the work very much easier. The best modern machine embroidery can be done on relatively unsophisticated machines. The emphasis of this book is the creative potential of your machine, not how many stitches can be stored in

1
Buying
A
Machine

its computer. The fully computerised machine may be great fun to use, but it is certainly not essential for creative machine embroidery.

The Needs of the Machine Embroiderer

This chapter will deal particularly with the needs of the creative embroiderer. Take time to research the subject thoroughly. Above all do not be content with a demonstration of a machine, but insist on using it yourself. Something as elementary as an uncomfortable foot control can be a disaster. If you already have a foot control that is difficult to use, consult your dealer. It is possible that you can have another make fitted, if the cycles are the same. Make sure it stops and starts smoothly and does not bounce off the table at full speed. A folded rug or purpose-made quilted mat will considerably reduce noise and vibration. Make sure your table is rigid.

Machine embroiderers are often dressmakers. Making original decorated clothing is one of the most satisfying (and possibly lucrative) uses of the craft. Generally speaking, machines that are good for dressmaking are also good for embroidery. They should do the basic dressmaking stitches, zigzag, running zigzag (serpentine), blind hemming, buttonholes, etc. Ideally there should be a roomful of machines: the *Bernina* for its reliability and easy controls; the *Elna* for its extensive range of automatic stitches and light balance wheel; the *Pfaff* for beautiful eyelets and even feed foot (so useful for patchworkers); the *White* (American) and the *New Home* (*Janome* in Australia) for their extra wide satin stitch. Since it's unlikely that the best features of each machine will ever be combined into one, you must compromise and buy the machine that offers the most features you need. Consider carefully what you are likely to do. If you are going to do garment construction with machine decoration, using neat presser-foot work, a varied range of automatic stitches would be useful. The capacity for carrying heavy or textured threads in the bobbin should also be a consideration, whereas, if you expect to work exclusively on big bold wall hangings, a basic zigzag and straight stitch machine would be adequate.

— Weight of Machines

Some machines are extremely heavy, others are light enough to be carried around comparatively easily. While weight should never be the main consideration, the fact remains that if your machine has to be removed from the dining room table for meals or must travel to workshops with you, awkward and bulky packing cases can be very inconvenient. However, lightweight machines are not recommended, except perhaps as a second machine; they are not fast enough generally and do not have sufficient surface area to support a large hoop. A projection-free, flat work surface is essential and the larger the better. It is important that there should be access to the bobbin without having to remove it. The machine embroiderer is likely to be changing bobbins far more frequently than the dressmaker.

— Machines that do not Embroider

Surprisingly, considering the spreading interest in machine embroidery, there are machines on the market that have neither a drop feed, nor a feed cover plate; in other words, they are not intended to do machine embroidery. While in some of them it is possible to remove the throat plate and replace it with washers beneath to raise its level, this would be too tedious to do frequently. If you already have one of these machines you have little option but to part-exchange it.

Presser foot satin stitch and free stitching, 25×26cm (9¾× 10¼in). The work was done very fast in a small hoop. The mind must run ahead of the needle to plan the curves. It would be very difficult to follow lines as complex as these; you must go with verve and hope for the best. The two-coloured satin stitch was done with the work upside down in the hoop; the outward flowing lines were added afterwards and, finally, the touches of free stitching.

'Sun on the Meadow' 21.5× 41cm (8×16in) is a slightly stylised landscape using every available shade of yellow and green in close straight stitch texture, bringing the bobbin thread to the surface.

Cardigan (sweater) Winter Anemones designed and worked by Tecla Miceli-Schulz of Brea, California. It is an adaptation from a design in a Dover book. Tecla teaches her students to work the design on a sheer fabric, such as polyester or silk organza, with Trace-a-pattern (a very thin stabiliser). When the main areas are stitched, the embroidery is applied to the garment, the edge is neatened and the stalks and other details are completed.

'Puss-on-Boots' by dj Bennett, Lake Forest, Illinois. They are embroidered with cable and straight stitching using silver and gold and other lustrous threads.

Mat by Margit Eisenbardt, Edmonton, Alberta. This beautiful mat, worked on an old Singer treadle machine, is a blend of hand and machine embroidery, which is time consuming and skilful work.

Slant Needle Machines

The slanting needle, once claimed to be a great innovation and used in quite recent machines, is a distinct disadvantage for the machine embroiderer. The hoop will move smoothly in the direction of the slant, but jerkily against it.

Needle Stop Up

Another recent innovation is the needle 'stop up'. This generally is more of an irritation than an advantage. In many of the stitch effects to be described in this book you will want to end a burst of stitching in a down position, as in satin stitch stars, or alternate right and left position for a double band of satin stitch beads. There is nothing more irritating than to stop stitching with the needle down and have to wait for it to come up, particularly if it rises slowly, when you immediately need to put it down again manually. We all managed extremely well previously without this gimmick. Most machines do not, as yet, have an optional release control, but the wiring can be disconnected. The embroiderer needs a needle that stops dead when the power is cut off, then she can flick the needle where required with the balance wheel.

The Bernina 1130 incorporates a 'needle stop down' control button, which largely overcomes the difficulty. If the needle stops on the wrong side, one tap on the back of the foot control will move it up, a second tap will take the needle to the opposite down position.

The Balance Wheel

The machine embroiderer is constantly using the balance wheel. One that is light to use is a must. If it is heavy, many of the effects described in this book will be difficult to execute. It is used for precision placing of satin stitch beads, and for applying beads and sequins. It is better than using the slow speed, because of the risk of damaging or breaking the needle, and it is more accurate.

Clearing the Race

All machine embroiderers will know how essential it is to lower the presser foot bar for free machining and how easy it is, however experienced you are, to forget it. Inevitably, sooner or later, you will jam the race. The so-called 'non-jamming races' of some machines are not foolproof. What is important is to know how to clear it. It is very rare indeed for jamming the race to throw out the timing of the machine, but it can happen. Be sensitive to any unusual noise in the machine, and stop quickly. It is usually easy to clear the race, but if the manual does not tell you how, be sure you are taught how to do it before you take a new machine home – but first check with your dealer that you will not invalidate the guarantee should you do so. In any case, it should come out for cleaning regularly as lint can get jammed underneath with extensive use. Thread snapping in an Elna is nearly always due to a thread, which may not be visible, caught in the race. Do not worry about losing the tiny screws; except in very old Elnas – they cannot fall out.

Talking Machines

There is a Japanese machine that exhorts one to 'please lower your presser foot'. It may cause general merriment in a workshop and embarrassment to its owner. Admittedly you would never jam the race from this cause, but I think most of us would prefer our machines to be silent.

Threading

Most modern machines thread easily, however, many have the thread inside the machine. The reel lies horizontally, held in position with a plastic cap. If you are used to an upright pin, it can be a real irritation removing and replacing this cap every time you change the colour. The top thread is also hidden in the workings of the machine so that you cannot get hold of it to test the tension. If the thread breaks, instead of just putting it back through the needle, it is sometimes necessary to rethread it from scratch because you cannot get hold of the end. This may seem a small point, but it could become a great irritation.

Bobbin Tension

The machine embroiderer frequently needs to alter the bobbin tension; this should be easy to do and ideally should be numbered. The embroiderer must completely understand and be able to alter both tensions quickly. Machines with separate bobbin cases have a slight advantage in that the user can have two or three bobbin cases suitably marked and set with different tensions. On the other hand, there is the disadvantage of a double movement every time the colour is changed – bobbin in case and case in machine. Bobbin cases with a flap instead of the notched tension spring are not so satisfactory for machine embroidery; the thread can disengage sideways.

— Covering or Dropping the Feed —

From the technical point of view there is little to choose between a drop feed and a cover plate. The raised cover plate creates a little extra tension on the fabric around the needle, which is good, but it also lessens the clearance between needle and plate, necessitating more care when removing and positioning the work. However, the hoop should slide under the needle quite easily while lying flat, provided the rings are level and that it is not more than 1cm (½in) deep. If the work is particularly thick, it is easy enough to slip the needle out, position the hoop and replace the needle without unthreading it. The Elna needle plate can be 'curved' by an engineer, obviating the need for a darning plate. This is particularly useful for open-work because threads can catch on the edge of the darning plate. Alternatively the feed, which is held on with two screws, can be removed, but you will need to buy the gauge for resetting it (H11005) and be shown how to use it. Quote your machine model when ordering. Singer, the only other machine to use a darning plate, needs no gauge to replace it.

— Eyelet Plate —

Eyelets are an important part of embroidery. At present, eyelet plates are made only for Elna, Bernina, Pfaff and Viking machines (Husquavarna in Australia). If it is expensive, consider it part of buying the machine. For those people who cannot do eyelets, imitation eyelets will be described later in the book. They are just as effective and can be any size, but they are slower to do.

— Stitch Width Control —

Lastly, the most important consideration of all. Does the machine have a control that opens and closes satin stitch and automatic stitches smoothly from a straight line to full width and back again? Whether you do this with or without the presser foot, lovely effects can be obtained and it is very sad if your machine cannot do it. The easiest way of controlling the stitch width is with a sliding lever or revolving knob, provided the variation is contained in half a revolution. In some older machines it is very difficult to turn the button without letting go of it halfway, thus losing the even flow of stitching. Sadly, some of the modern machines have made

this operation difficult. The stitch is widened by pressing a button several times to get from 0 to full width, and pressing another button to decrease it. If you want to work small petal shapes of satin stitch, it is barely possible to operate the button pressing fast enough. The problem is made even worse by the fact that most electronic machines have only thirteen steps when increasing the stitch width. The result of this is that tapering satin stitch has noticeable steps in it. The simple lever offers even widening and narrowing, swiftly or very slowly.

Bernina's new range of electronic machines (1130) appear to have overcome this problem. They have light, dialled stitch width control, and fifty-one steps from 0 to full width. The result is a perfect taper. Incidentally, they run at 1,050 stitches per minute at full speed and stop faster than any other machine, with the needle up or down, instantly. This completely overcomes the problem mentioned earlier, and it is the only machine that can do it as yet. Sadly, not all manufacturers consider the embroiderer and, while we are an ever increasing body of people, we have so far failed to influence them. It seems we will have to wait a while for the universal return of the stitch width lever.

— Care of Your Machine —

If you use your machine daily, do get it checked every 18 months; neglected maladjustments can become expensive. Motor brushes should be checked regularly.

Even though the instruction manuals say your machines do not need oiling, remember that the parts during manufacture are cooled in oil, thus absorbing some, which is shed to lubricate the machine during use. Commonsense tells us that the supply is not inexhaustible. Wherever two pieces of metal work against each other, a drop of oil will do no harm and most certainly will help to prolong the life of your machine. The operative word is 'a drop'. If too much oil is used, there is risk of oil splashing onto the motor and damaging it. However, never oil a computer machine except where instructed. This advice comes, not from me, but from my trusted machine dealer and expert.

Finally, when you buy your machine make use of any free lessons offered and be sure that you will receive good follow-up service and help when you need it.

These are the main points to consider before buying a sewing machine. Technology is changing so fast that this chapter may well need updating by the time this book gets to print.

'The Dancer' by Ros Chilcot. This work shows a very textural approach. Many scraps of nets and other sheer fabrics are held down with many rows of zigzag.

2
Equipment
And
Materials

— Types of Hoops —

Apart from attachments and machine accessories, the most important piece of equipment is your hoop. It must have a screw adjustment, be well fitting and strong and narrow enough to pass under your needle with the darning (embroidery) plate in position (Elna and Singer). Spring metal hoops do not hold the work tightly enough, and there is no support for the fabric at all between the handles, and the groove is not deep enough to allow for appliqué or heavy fabric. They are useful only for darning, signing the work, etc. Plastic hoops are not satisfactory; they are too flexible and slippery, some of them have a ridge on the lower edge of the outer ring that prevents the work from moving smoothly and the fabric from making close contact with the machine. Very narrow but deep wooden hoops are not strong enough, and the metal fittings bend too easily. Otherwise most wooden hoops are satisfactory.

— Correcting Ill Fitting Hoops —

When you buy a hoop, hold it up to the light with the screw finger tight, so that you can see whether it fits well all the way round. Often the ends of the outer ring point in too sharply, making spaces on each side; this can be corrected by filing the points. Bind the inner ring of the hoop as tightly as possible with cotton tape, bias or seam binding; a clothes peg will help to hold the first couple of turns. If it is not done properly, the pressure exerted to engage the two rings will soon dislodge the tape. To prevent your roll of tape unwinding and getting out of control, use a pin and unwind the roll a foot at a time. Finally stitch the finishing end on top of, or inside, the inner ring to avoid extra bulk between the rings. For very fragile fabrics prepare a special hoop with both inner and outer rings bound, using the finest available tape. If you use a strong colour, you are less likely to lose your hoop in a workshop. Take care with the choice and preparation of your hoops; the success of your work depends on cloth stretched to its maximum in a perfectly fitting hoop. No machine can function without some tension on the threads. In the absence of the presser foot there is nothing to counteract the strain but the tightness of the work.

— Repairing Hoops —

Hoops do not last for ever. So much pressure is exerted on the outer ring that, with continual use, splitting may occur near the screw fitting. The strength of modern woodwork adhesives makes it worthwhile repairing them. The join will need to be glued and clamped. Many hoops in America have particularly sharp edges. The method of framing (which is an excellent one) described in the next paragraph will be much easier if the outer edges of the inner ring are curved slightly with a wood file, and there will be less risk of damage to fine fabrics.

— Framing Firm Fabrics —

Always stand up to stretch the fabric with the work flat on the table. Adjust the screw so that you need to use half your weight to engage it (if you can do this sitting down the screw won't be tight enough). With the fabric right side up (except for cable stitch) laid over the outer ring, lay the inner ring on top. First push the edge down on the far side of the hoop. Bring the pressure round the sides and with the heels of both hands lean heavily on the near edge to push it down. With the outer edges of

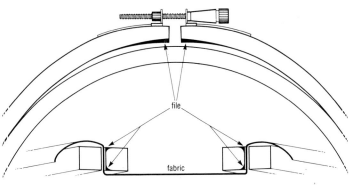

Fig 1 *A fault in the hoop and how to correct it by filing inner points (blackened on diagram) of the outer ring. To slightly curve the outer edges of the inner hoop facilitates stretching the fabric.*

'Bud', a simple but effective, use of straight stitch using line and texture. The latter has contrasting coloured bobbin thread showing on the surface (see colour sample on p23).

your palms resting on the sides of the hoop to prevent it springing apart, use thumbs and forefingers to pull the fabric upward and inwards. This is the only way to get sufficient leverage to pull the work tight. Keep turning the hoop so that you always tighten on the part of the hoop nearest to you. Concentrate on keeping both warp and weft threads straight. Continue until there is no more give in the fabric.

— Framing Fragile and Silky Fabric —

If you use the method just described, you will find that the fabric will get damaged by the hoop, so the method must be modified. This method also works well on fabrics with above average bias stretch, which can make it difficult to lay them straight on the hoop. Start with the hoop very loose, only just tight enough to hold the fabric, so that it is easy to pull the fabric straight both ways without damaging it. Progress cautiously, alternately tightening the work and tightening the screw. When tightening the

work, instead of tugging with thumbs and forefingers, use all your fingers to even the strain along both palms. This method will all but eliminate the dislodging of threads in the fabric. For fine silk, it is wise to keep a special hoop with both inner and outer ring tightly bound. With patience, the most fragile of fabrics can be pulled drum tight, and drum tight they must be.

— Framing Tulle and Plastic Mesh —

Some fabrics such as tulle or fine fabric mesh cannot be tightened once they are in the hoop, therefore the work must be stretched before the inner ring is pushed down. Ideally two people should hold the fabric stretched for you while you engage the inner ring, or you can set up an elaborate system of weights, irons, typewriters, etc, all the way round, or you can pin the fabric to a foam or cork board, remembering to put the outer ring under the fabric first. However, it is possible to do it alone without going to such lengths. My demonstration of this causes general amusement. Find a waist-high work surface, such as in the kitchen, and allow plenty of fabric round the hoop. The screw should be fairly tight. With hoop and fabric in position, place the lower edge of the fabric over the edge of the kitchen surface and support it with your stomach. With your right hand, pull the left edge away from you, stretching it, then support it with your left forearm and bend your wrist inwards to hold half the far edge. With downward and outward pressure of right forearm and hand, stretch the fabric as much as you can. Then lean your whole torso firmly on the work, press the inner ring down with your thumbs, gradually working your hands down the edge, until you can press the ring down finally by your stomach. It is surprising just how tight this method can get the work. I used it successfully for a stole with applied yarns on tulle.

Finally let it be stressed again, it is vital to frame properly; there is no substitute for tight work.

— Testing for Tightness —

In spite of all exhortations, the average beginner does not get the work as tight as it should be. There are simple tests that you can apply to find out whether you have done a good job. You should not be able to dislodge the rings between your thumb and forefinger, nor should you be able to move the fabric inside the hoop when gripping it an inch or two from the edge.

— Needles

During normal sewing with the presser foot, the pull on the needle is downwards; while machine embroidering the pull is in any and every direction, so obviously the strength of the needle is less important when doing regular sewing. Except on very fine silks or polyesters use a 90 needle, which will not bend if jerked or pulled. If a needle bends, the machine will miss stitches; the needle may also break on the edge of the plate. This is more likely to happen at medium or slow speeds. I once gave a workshop on Elna Lotus machines in a country district; no one had any 90 needles, only 70s. One after another broke. There was no alternative: someone had to drive to the nearest town to buy some, after which there was no more trouble. The problem was aggravated because portable machines do not run as fast as full size ones. It brought home to everyone the importance of a strong needle, regardless of the thickness of the thread being used. With a really strong needle you can safely move the hoop very fast to make long stitches, which look quite different from short ones; exciting textures can be made also by moving the hoop in a series of jerks. Both effects should be done with the motor at maximum speed. Larger needles make more noise piercing the fabric, this is unavoidable. Ball point needles are not necessary but your regular needle must be sharp; try a ball point needle though, if your fabric is snagging.

With a 90 needle it is possible to make very long stitches which catch the light, whereas short ones tend to sink into the fabric, giving a more subdued effect. Another advantage of a 90 needle is that any thread up to 40 weight sewing cotton can be used without changing it. Buy good quality needles, preferably ones recommended by the manufacturers, rather than cheap ones from the supermarket. It is interesting to test their flexibility; quality does vary. The embroiderer would prefer a rigid needle; they have to be made flexible though, for safety reasons, so that they snap rather than shatter.

Twin and triple needles can be used for free embroidery; they are literally two needles clamped together. There are different sizes; the wider the gap, the narrower any satin stitching must be. Test the width by turning the balance wheel before positioning the work.

— Attachments and Accessories

Useful attachments, sold as extras, are eyelet plates, fagotting bar, embroidery foot, braiding or couching foot, multiple braider, fringe or tailor tacking foot and circular sewing bar. The use of these will be covered in chapter 11.

You need a large supply of bobbins, which are best kept, closely packed on their sides so that the colours can be seen, in a flat box. An Elna rug fork and a Viking weaver's reed can also be useful accessories.

— Fabrics

Almost any fabric can be used for machine embroidery but rigid ones make the best backgrounds. Stretch fabrics need to be supported during working. This can be done with a layer of thin fabric on the back for free machining, or on paper when using the presser foot or iron-on Vilene. The latter method is not generally recommended because it stiffens the work. This is acceptable on certain parts of a garment such as belts, hats, cuffs, collars, etc, but on a draping skirt or table cloth it is best avoided. For work meant to be heirlooms it is wise to avoid as many chemical substances as possible as it is impossible to foresee what adverse effects they may have on your work in years to come. It is better to be safe than sorry. Do not use them; stay with old-fashioned methods of marking out, tack and pin rather than glue.

When you machine embroider a garment, always buy a little extra fabric to test it with the stitch techniques that you hope to use, particularly if you intend doing a lot of satin stitch. Some of the lighter weight cottons and poly cottons will not support satin stitch without puckering however tight they are in the hoop, and a stabiliser may be needed. It may be possible to work largely with straight stitch effects and only small amounts of narrow satin stitch. Remember that when all satin stitch lines converge to one point, as in a flower centre, there is the greatest risk of distortion. Work with upper and lower tensions as loose as possible to minimise pulling up. A lightweight backing may cure the distortion, but it will stiffen the work and will show through semi-transparent work, and may take a lot of time to trim back to the stitching. It is wisest to restrict the design to the limitations of the cloth, or to choose a fabric with enough substance to support the stitching.

The machine is a superb drawing instrument; to show fine machining at its best, use finely woven fabric. Heavy weaves can make a distracting geometric texture, and such fabrics are better used for applied yarns and heavy appliqué and drawn thread work. Very open fabrics, such as butter muslin, net, scrim, plastic mesh, are fun to work on;

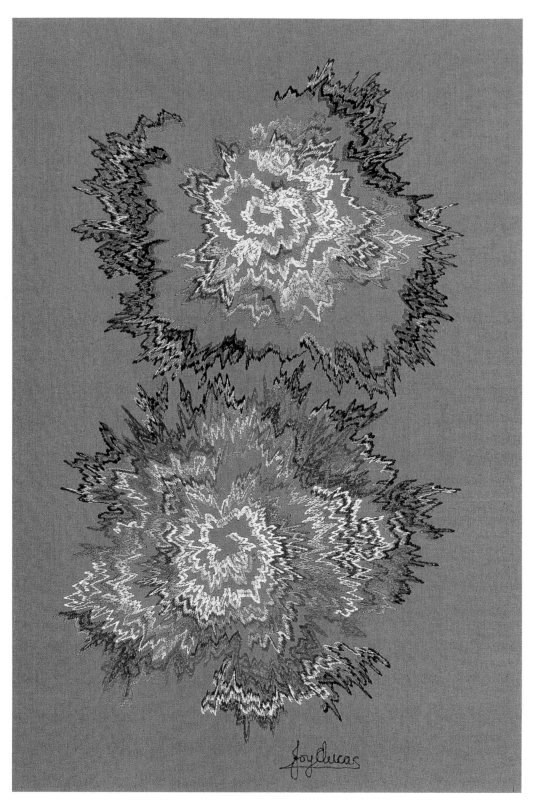

'Forces' is stitched throughout with a twin needle, often using a variegated thread in one needle and a blending plain colour in the other. The satin stitch must (depending on the gap between the needles) be narrow enough to avoid hitting the side of the needle hole.

18

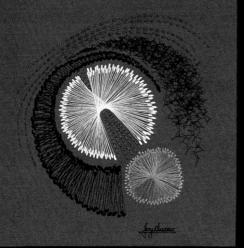

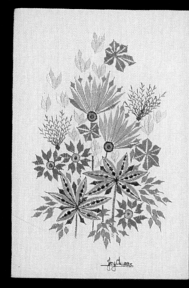

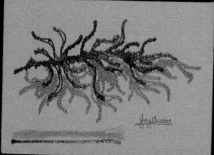

threads can be pulled out, cut and forced to one side or the other, and the removed threads can be reapplied in tufts or fringes.

The effect of machine embroidery on velvet is quite different from any other fabric. Hoop marks can generally be removed with a steaming kettle and a soft toothbrush.

Look at all fabrics and threads and everything in your home with an appraising eye. It is amazing what the innovative person can use in embroidery, from tin foil to tap washers.

— Threads

Machine embroidery thread is manufactured in many parts of the world. There is a great variety in rayon thread, which is more widely used commercially than cotton. In Britain we are familiar with Natesh (Indian) and Madeira Sticku, and the very fine Toledo monogramming thread (West Germany). Also obtainable in various parts of America and Australia are Fiocolor, Mez Alcazar, Isafil and Mexpoli to name a few. Most of them are excellent; they are tightly spun, fine and smooth. The less satisfactory kind is barely spun at all and looks like floss. These will break in the needle but may be used in the bobbin. They are most likely to be found in Granny's ottoman! Whenever you are purchasing any new brand of thread, buy one only to test. If it breaks, it really needs to be discarded. Rayon thread has a high lustre compared to cotton. Only you can decide whether the extreme shininess is appropriate for your work. You will find that, unless you are doing very close satin stitch, the shine is less obvious than you would imagine. Rayon thread has more stretch in it than cotton, so it is not suitable for use with a tight tension.

Machine embroidery cotton, while not so shiny as rayon thread, has a greater lustre than normal sewing thread. There is a wide range of colours in DMC (French) both variegated and plain, in two thicknesses, 30 and 50 denier, the latter being the finer and most useful. The range is deficient only in muted grey blues and dull mauves and greens. The 30 weight is so similar to 50 sewing cotton it is not worth buying, at least not to start with; most of us who sew regularly will have a good supply of them already. However if you have to sew many yards of satin stitch it will be accomplished in much less time using 30 on top than 50. Otherwise, the most common cotton machine embroidery thread to be found in Britain is the Swedish Molnlycke. It is a beautiful, lustrous 40 weight thread, and although the colour range is limited, it offers some that are missing in the DMC range. Clark's range is less extensive than DMC. The Swiss Mettler has a wide range containing some very subtle colours missing from the others. Having said that these threads are available in Britain, there is comparatively little demand and it will be necessary to get them from a specialised shop or machine dealer.

The extremely fine monofilament nylon thread, used in the clothing industry, makes a very smooth satin stitch if used with a very light tension, and it is very cheap since a large cone lasts for so long. As it is too large to stand on the thread pin, stand it behind the machine below the normal position, pass the end through a hole on the top of a bobbin placed on the thread pin. Then thread normally. If the thread pin is inside the machine, tape or tie a bobbin to the top of the machine and pass the thread through it, or else wind a bobbin and use it as a reel. Otherwise use your imagination; there is always a way. This thread can be used in the bobbin for extensive satin stitch when the bobbin thread is not to be seen; a finer thread underneath ensures a close stitch without fear of jamming the feed and causing the work to get stuck under the foot.

Cotton thread, whilst being reliable from the breaking point of view, can get brittle with age or if it becomes too dry. If it snaps easily in your hand, it will probably do so during stitching. It can be strengthened by steaming over boiling water. Failing that, run the top layer off onto a bobbin, where, not being subjected to the same stress as the top thread, it will probably cause no trouble. The underneath thread, which has not been exposed to air, should be in good condition.

To give variety to your work it is important to have a selection of many types and thicknesses of thread. The fineness of 50 DMC and thin rayon thread is much more satisfactory for all satin effects than the heavier sewing threads, which do not give a smooth effect and tend to jam the eyelet plate. Except for special effects, which will be described later, always use fine thread underneath. It is cheaper, you can get more on your bobbin, and everything works more smoothly.

Transparent thread, both light and dark, can be used for sewing on fabric and yarns when an exact match of thread is not available. It has a rich glint, giving a wonderful texture for free stitching. A very special effect occurs when the bobbin tension is loosened to allow loops of the under thread to come to the surface. Do not, however, use it on the back of the work because, if it comes in contact with your iron, it will melt. Always press the work on the wrong side.

Fine silk thread is available (Japanese) but it is expensive. Again, try it before you invest in a large number of reels. There are available in most good sewing shops a number of silver, gold and metallic coloured threads that work well in the needle.

A collection should be made of all kinds of thick thread for the applied yarn technique and cable stitch (heavy thread in the bobbin). These include hand embroidery threads, knitting and weaving yarns, rug wool, plastic string, sisal, etc. Textured threads can be pulled off heavy suiting remnants and tweeds. Bias strips, ribbons and cords can also be used.

— Stabilisers

Stabilisers and interfacings have been flooding onto the market recently. They are used to give support to thin fabrics and knits during free embroidery. There are crisp and soft ones, and others that are slightly flexible. There is a fabric that dissolves in boiling water, and a plastic that dissolves in cold; there is even a soluble paper. Their usefulness varies; generally the crisp ones are the best, but a method will be described later where paper is used instead. The dissolving paper eliminates the argument that 'the stabiliser stiffens the work'. Many of these, though, are available only in America where interest in machine embroidery is enormous and growing rapidly. Dissolving plastic (Aqua-Solv or Solvy in America) has unlimited potential. Techniques, which have hitherto been difficult and time consuming, have been made very much easier. Buy small quantities of stabilisers at first, and test them thoroughly before use. If one does not suit your purpose, try another.

Before soluble plastic and fabric came on the market, vanishing muslin was used for machine embroidered lace and stabilising fabric. It is a brittle fabric that crumbles under a hot iron and, because of the heat, only cotton thread could be used. It was a time consuming task removing shreds from the finished work.

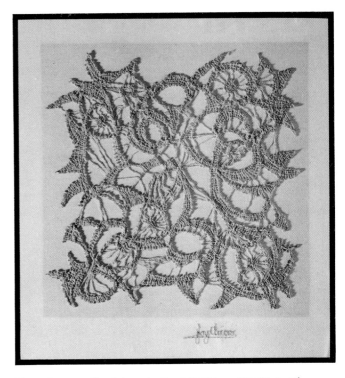

Linen lace on dissolving plastic, 24×24cm (9×9in). The linen thread broke repeatedly. Notice how everything connects.

Another example of lace worked on dissolving plastic with silver thread, 14.5×16cm (5¾×6¼in). Notice how some edges are satin stitched for support and effect.

21

Stitch samples

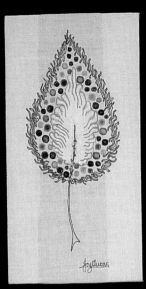

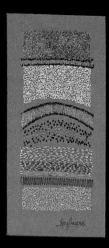

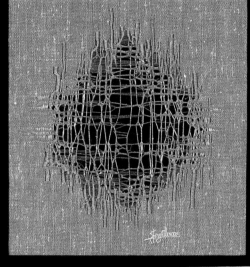

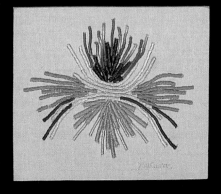

— Working Position —

A comfortable working position is vital, and this is not the same as for regular sewing. Machine tables are often too low. You should work sitting on a chair that allows your thighs to be parallel to the ground; any hollowed-out seats that cause the spine to curve should be filled with a cushion. Your back should be straight and the bed of the machine at bust level. Tension in the neck and shoulders will be reduced if the body is supported, with the left elbow on the table or machine, while the right hand guides the work, most of the time from the shoulder. There is not enough flexibility in the wrist joint for anything but very short lines or close textures. The left hand should exert slight downward pressure on the hoop to help steady it. On a large hoop it helps to lay the hand with the little finger and outer side of the palm against the edge. The thumb and third or fourth finger (according to the size of the hoop) of the right hand should push the hoop away and the remaining fingers should be on the fabric inside the hoop to steady it, and vice versa when the hoop is pulled. In lino cutting the worker will use the left hand to steady the cutting hand to prevent it slipping and cutting too much; the principle here is the same, the steadying process makes control much easier.

Sitting, with your back straight and your left elbow supported, slightly curtails the distance between your eyes and the needle. If this causes a problem, it is worth getting special glasses.

— Stretching the Work —

This chapter is for beginners and the less experienced machine embroiderers. The basic procedures are covered in most machine manuals and other books on the subject. Nevertheless, a few reminders will not come amiss; there may even be a few useful hints for the more experienced.

When learning, choose a firm fabric, such as cotton or poly cotton. Stretch it in a wooden hoop with a screw adjustment. If it is not evenly gripped and does not feel and sound like a drum when tapped, refer to the instructions for framing in chapter 2.

3
Free Machine Embroidery

The success of your work from the technical point of view depends on the background fabric being stretched to its maximum. No machine can work without some tension on upper and lower thread. Without the support of the presser foot there is only the tension of the fabric to withstand it.

— Preparing the Machine —

Remove the presser foot and shank (if your machine has clip-on feet). If left on, the shank may catch in any raised stitching. Drop the feed, or fit the darning and embroidery plate, as described in the machine manual. Learn with a 90/14 needle. Many beginners use fine thread and an appropriately fine needle. Lack of skill may cause them to be jerky in their movements of the hoop. A sudden jerk on a fine needle will bend it, causing the machine to miss stitches; at worst the needle may break. This risk is all but eliminated with the stronger needle. It can carry any weight of thread up to 40 sewing cotton. It is a good idea to practise using fine thread right from the start. Use different colours above and below (both of which contrast with the background). You will begin to appreciate the exciting and varied effects that occur by changing tensions and the size of the stitch. Always thread with the presser foot bar up to ensure that the thread goes fully into the tension discs (but remember then to lower it).

— Positioning the Hoop —

With the needle in its highest position, slide the hoop under it, taking care to spread the fabric out so that the edges do not get caught underneath in the stitching.

On Elnas, the needle clearance is restricted by the plate. Provided that your hoop does not exceed 1cm (½in), and it is not excessively heavily bound, it will go under. Be sure that inner and outer rings are level. Do not tilt the hoop, or be impatient and force it if it does not immediately clear the needle, as it will damage the point. Elna owners may like to file a hollow in the hoops to facilitate positioning. For people with slant needle machines it is obviously sensible to position the hoop from behind. The surface of the material should be flat against the machine. It should not be necessary to say this, but occasionally someone will put the hoop under the needle upside down, with disastrous results.

— Starting to Stitch —

It may be helpful for beginners to remember that there are three things to check once the work is in position but before stitching:

1 Draw the bobbin thread up through the fabric so that it does not tangle in the subsequent stitching. It is not necessary to pull it to the surface of the machine first. Holding the work down with your left index finger will ensure that it comes up easily.
2 Lower the presser foot bar. Without the presser foot it is easily forgotten. It sets the top tension, so forgetting it will cause the top threads to loop and jam the machine.
3 Support both threads under your finger while you start stitching. If you do not, a loop of thread will get caught below the machine and tangle.

Once the stitching has gripped the fabric, the ends can be cut at a convenient moment. Practise, running the machine at a medium speed. Try to follow a line and machine round shapes a second time; write your name. It all helps you to gain control. It is illogical because it is tantamount to moving paper under a pencil, but you will soon get used to it. Turn the work to any angle to make full use of the hoop, but do not as yet try to do that while you are stitching.

— Stitch Length —

A frequent question is 'what stitch length should I use?' Your stitch length control is best at 0. The stitch length is determined by how quickly you move the hoop in relation to the machine's motor speed. If running it at a constant speed, the faster you move the hoop the longer the stitch.

On an Elna, a stitch length of 3 or more can cause the feed to hit the darning plate; maximum length will dislodge it. (One stitch turning the balance wheel by hand at full length is the official way to remove the plate.) On other machines, wherever the length control is set cannot affect the stitching, since the feed is either covered or below the bed of the machine. You decide the stitch length by co-ordinating the motor speed and the speed at which you move the hoop.

Free automatic stitching, 20.5×20.5cm (8×8in), including free running zigzag, blind hemming and pattern 3 on the Elna air electronic. Either a black or white bobbin was used with a slightly loosened under-tension allowing the thread to come through to the top. It is mounted so that it can be seen from either side.

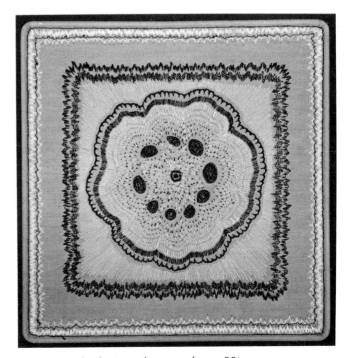

The reverse side of 5 (see colour sample on p22)

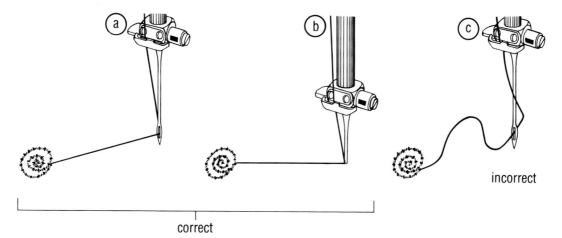

a   b   c

incorrect

correct

Fig 2 *How to move from one area to another: tension must be maintained on the thread; if too much thread has been pulled through, it is necessary to pull up the bobbin loop and support both threads while starting to stitch.*

— Moving From One Shape to the Next —

When a shape is complete, raise the needle bar to its highest position and lift the presser foot bar to release the top tension. Move the hoop to the new position, lowering the needle into the fabric with the balance wheel. Lower the presser foot and continue stitching.

— Finishing the Ends —

When you trim, cut the ends and connecting threads closely on top, then on the back, leaving 0.5cm (¼in) ends. The slight pull exerted in doing this beds the top ends down firmly in the fabric.

Since there is no pull on the fabric and if the tensions are approximately balanced the stitching will not come undone. Even so it is wise, as an extra precaution, to do very small stitches at the beginnings and ends of lines. If you have ever had to unpick minute stitching you will appreciate just how secure they can be!

For safety's sake, do not touch your power control until you are ready to stitch; train yourself to take your foot off every time you stop.

— The Darning Foot —

Some machine manuals will suggest that you fit the darning foot in place of the presser foot for free machining. It's a spring-loaded foot that connects with the needle bar, thus raising and lowering it with every stitch. This enables the work to be moved smoothly under the needle, but the work is held down at the critical moment when the top thread loop is passing the underside of the bobbin case, making it impossible for the work to lift and causing missed stitching. It is a safety measure for young children and it can be useful for quilting and machining through several layers of fabric. If the work is as tight as it should be, and you use your fingers to hold it down should it tend to lift, there is no need at all to use it. If you are doing particularly heavy work involving layers of furnishing fabrics, which would be too thick to go in a hoop, the darning foot can be used without the hoop, which is an alternative way of working. If the fabrics are both heavy and rigid, a backing may not be necessary. If, because of arthritis or any other reason, you are unable to get the hoop tight, it could be the answer. Generally, better results are obtained on fine fabrics with the hoop, but with all the new stabilisers on the market, the degree of pulling up under zigzag and satin stitch will be minimised.

Some machines will tolerate the slight lifting of the work during stitching, some older ones will not, making it necessary to place your fingers near the needle (or to use the darning foot). It is better to work without it, if possible, because it is not so easy to see what you are doing, and the foot going up and down may be hard on the eyes. However, in cases of technical difficulty, when everything else has been checked, always try it. It can cure thread breaking and can be helpful for openwork.

— Tensions —

If you are using normal thread, you can work at normal tensions; very thin thread requires a light tension. The general principle is to loosen the tension gradually if the thread breaks, until you find the point at which it does not. Remember, though, that you must always have some tension. Too loose a top tension has the same result as forgetting to lower the presser foot bar. The top thread is under more

26

'Autumn Blaze' is worked with closely packed free zigzag, changing the angle of the stitching continuously.

'Bella' by Enid Gratton Guinness. Enid calls this her 'apprentice' piece. It is densely worked straight stitching in every available shade in her colour range.

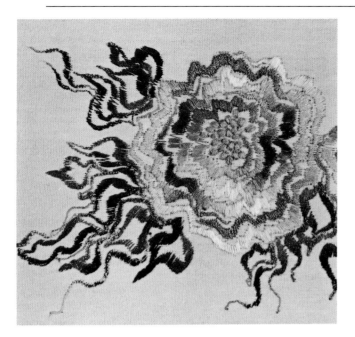

Free satin stitching, 23 × 13cm (9¼ × 5in), using variegated thread; there are small satin stitch beads in the flower centres (see colour sample on p19).

stress than the bobbin thread because of the action of the take up lever and the number of pressure points the thread goes through. Bobbin thread breaking is very much less likely because it has merely a 0.5cm (¼in) travel before it emerges from the tension spring. Because of these factors, a finer than normal thread in the bobbin will slip through more easily making it unnecessary, from the breaking point of view, to loosen it.

— Varying Threads, Thicknesses and Tensions –

There are three rules for the seamstress, all of which can be broken for machine embroidery. First, use the same thread on top and in the bobbin; secondly, the same colour; and thirdly, the use of balanced tensions. Within these three variables there is a whole range of exciting effects. These can also be combined with automatic stitching. It is fun to experiment. The important thing is not that you should have balanced tensions, but that you can alter them for any desired effect and put them back quickly. People with bobbin case machines often like to have two bobbin cases, one for regular dressmaking and one for embroidery.

— Free Zigzag and Automatic Stitches

Satin stitch and all automatic stitches based on the side-to-side needle swing, but not any involving the reverse feed action (simply because the feed is below machine level and therefore not operating), can be used freely. Free machining with full width satin stitch is a bit like drawing with an italic nib. When you move the hoop backwards and forwards, the stitch is wide and sideways narrow. Shaping can be accomplished by revolving the hoop; it is sometimes called directional tapering.

— Top Thread Breaking

The most common problems are thread breaking, which occurs mostly on top, and missing stitches. The latter is the most easily cured; it is nearly always due to the work not being drum tight in the hoop. The further from the edge of the hoop you are stitching the more likely it is that the work will lift as the needle rises. Press material in the hoop lightly with your left hand.

Breaking top thread, assuming that it is in good condition and not brittle, may be due to too tight a top tension, a fault in the threading (for instance, an extra turn round a thread guide), or less often a burr on the edge of the plate, or faults or knots in the thread. When using very fine thread the principle is to release the top tension gradually until the point where it does not break is found. Never release the tension completely.

— Lower Thread Breaking

Breaking of the lower thread is not so easily cured and can mean a burr on the hook. These can be more easily felt with the edge of your nail than seen. If one is found, rub it smooth very gently with the finest grade of emery paper. Also check the needle slots on machine and darning plate; they can be smoothed with a see-sawing action using a strip of fine emery cut to fit.

In some machines a build-up of fluff under the bobbin tension spring can cause breaking; so can even the smallest piece of cotton lodged, perhaps invisibly, in the race, which should be removed and cleaned regularly. When a bobbin is wound, the thread should be passed through the hole in the top of it and held clear while the bobbin is winding until it snaps off or is cut. Inattention may cause it to go over the edge and get caught in the winding. This is easily overlooked and will cause continual breaking.

If a machine misses an occasional stitch, even when the work is fully stretched, or tends to miss one side of a zigzag, it may mean that the timing is going out of adjustment, in which case take it to your dealer.

Many exciting stitch effects are obtained by varying tensions and using different colours and thicknesses of threads on top and in the bobbin. Forget all the rules learned in your dressmaking classes and experiment.

— Whip Stitch —

This is a beautiful stitch. Although it is a straight stitch, it is raised and looks very much more solid than free running. The tensions are adjusted so that the top thread lies flat on the surface pulling up loops of bobbin thread to cover it. To set your machine, choose fine machine embroidery thread, a 50 DMC or the fine Natesh rayon thread for the bobbin, and a heavy sewing cotton for the top, which, while you are learning, should contrast with both the fabric and bobbin colours. The bobbin tension should be a little less than normal. With fine thread underneath, which slips through more easily, it may not be necessary to change it. Heavier threads can be used underneath but they will definitely have to be loosened. The top tension should be at or near maximum, which is why strong cotton is better than rayon, as it will not stretch. Use a 90 needle. The machine should be run very fast and the hoop moved slowly so that the loops of the under thread are so close that they conceal the top thread. Perfect whip stitch should be a smooth raised line of the bobbin colour. If an uneven line results, with small loops of the top thread breaking out between the loops from the bobbin, it means that the top thread is not tight enough. However, if you are already at maximum, you must loosen the under tension instead until the stitch is perfect. If the top thread breaks, both tensions must be set lower but in the same relationship to each other. As a last resort, with persistent breaking, try a good quality polyester thread – some stretch more than others.

— Whip Stitch Variations —

The uneven effect described above can be done on purpose, making a very attractive textured line. Try loosening the top tension to normal or less. On a loosely woven cloth you may find loops of the top thread going through to the back. If this is exciting

4

Stitch Effects

enough it can become the front by turning the work upside down in the hoop.

Another variation results from moving the hoop fast. This makes gaps between the loops of bobbin thread, exposing the top thread. It looks like a fine hand couched line. While running the machine at a constant speed, any sharp change of direction in the stitched line will cause a build up of bobbin loops because you cannot avoid slowing the hoop. These can be accentuated with a brief pause. A wonderful texture can be made by moving the hoop in a series of pauses and jerks; the machine must be run at full speed or you may break your needle. The hoop can also be moved gradually increasing and decreasing the speed to give a gently changing colour line.

— Whip Stitch and Automatic Stitching —

Whip stitch tensions and contrasting coloured threads used with automatic stitching are well worth exploring. The straight parts of the automatic stitch will be bobbin coloured and the swing the top colour. Try them also releasing both tensions with fine thread on top. Remember that automatic stitches (though not reverse feed stitches) can be done freely, adding a whole new dimension to the craft for textured fillings. Turn the work over, it is often very exciting on the back; if you like what you see, mount the work upside down. Work, exciting on both sides, can be mounted in a hoop or square metal frame and be seen either way. Instructions for mounting will be given in a later chapter.

When you have set perfect whip stitch tensions on your machine, note the settings, or at least memorise the resistance you feel when you pull both threads. All whip stitch ends should be pulled to the back by exerting pressure on the lower thread and cutting 0.5cm (¼in) from the work.

When stitching whip stitch spirals (see p.30) the ends can be pulled through if you cut the top thread of every circle, as you work, after two or three rounds of stitching. When you turn the work over, the top thread will come through when the bobbin thread is pulled. Pull the outer end of the first circle through, working in the correct sequence following the bobbin thread.

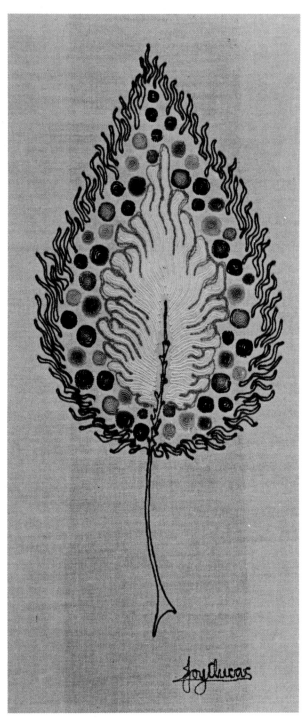

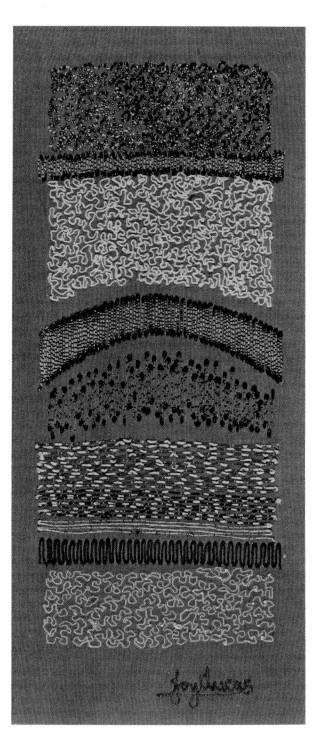

Whip stitch, 12×23cm (4¾×9in); the spirals are worked with variegated thread. Always work them from the inside (see colour sample on p23).

Whip stitch variations, 9×19cm (3½×7½in). The top band is worked with a light tension to give a varied textural line. Notice the bobbin colour build-up on the change of direction. The straight two-coloured band with a white bobbin was worked by moving the hoop in pauses and jerks. The lowest band was worked from the wrong side and demonstrates the difference in the weight of the 50 DMC thread used in the bobbin and the upper white band worked from the front with 40 sewing cotton through the needle (see sample on p23).

'The Burghead Bull' by Jennifer Wilson, 56×39cm (15.25× 22in). The design is based on an ancient Pictish stone carving discovered at Burghead – the bull stands out against a background that gives an impression of his native Morayshire coast and the flora therein. 'As a first step the background fabric (calico) was painted with inks. The bull, in a rough silk fabric, was appliquéd to the background, using machine satin stitch, and then painted with ink. The background, except for the sky, was entirely filled in with machine stitching, using whip stitch, running and satin stitches.'   Jennifer Wilson

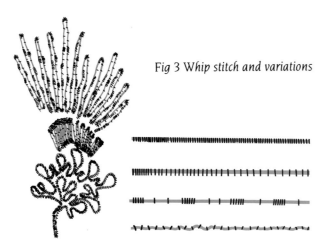

Fig 3 Whip stitch and variations

'Kani' by Jennie Abbott, Perth, Australia. Jennie worked the frill for this frilled neck lizard in my first workshop in Australia. I wrote to her to ask to see the finished product; I wasn't disappointed. She has done other beautiful wild life subjects. In this piece, she has used crinkle taffeta with whip stitching to create the scaly texture. The frill is wired to show the defensive posture. Height 25cm (10in); length 60cm (2ft); frill 30cm (12in).   Joy Clucas

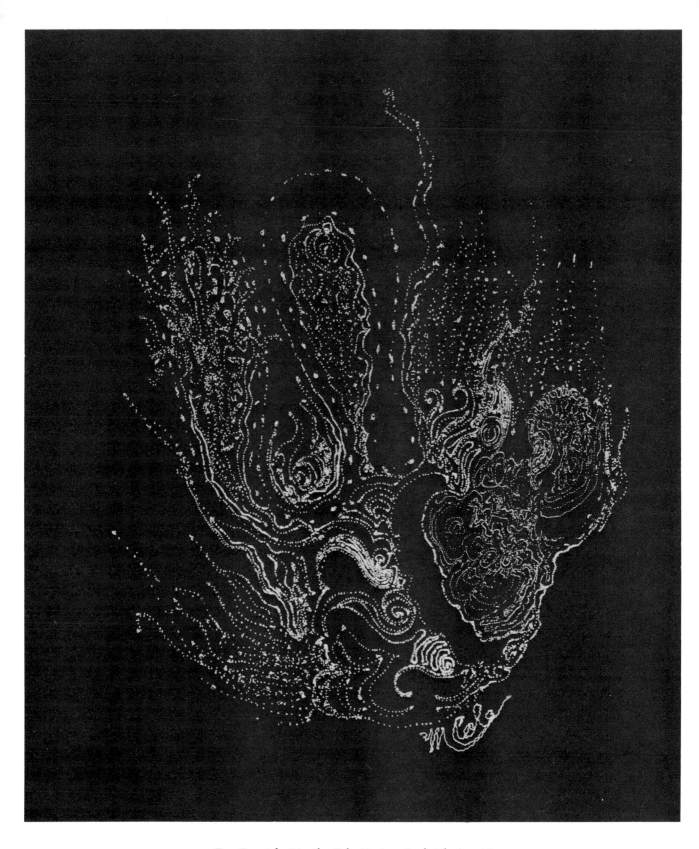

'Free Form' by Martha Cole, Regina, Saskatchewan, 19×
22.5cm (7½×9in). This delightful delicate embroidery is a
varied whip stitch line with white bobbin and black top thread
throughout.

— Unreliable Top Tension —

On some machines at maximum tension you may suddenly see the top thread instead of the bobbin thread. If you pull the top thread you will feel that there is no tension even though the foot is down. Unless you stop very quickly you will spoil your work. Lift and lower the presser foot bar, that may reset it, if not, reduce the tension to nothing and tighten it up again, you will feel it reset itself. If this happens frequently you must reduce the upper tension to the point where it does not happen and adjust the bottom tension to it. This occurs on some Berninas and occasionally on Vikings and Pfaffs. It is never critical if the tensions are a bit higher or lower so long as they are in the correct relationship to each other. You must discover new tricks to get what you need. If more than maximum tension is needed on top, you can pass the thread round the second thread pin a couple of times. The Elna Carina tensions are sometimes set slightly tighter than on other machines. If less top tension is required because of excessive pulling up, the presser foot bar can be left up. If there is still too much tension, rethread, but miss out the tension wheel (situated on top of the machine) and the first thread guide. Try this on any machine. If the resulting stitches are too loose, create a little extra tension by taking a turn round the second thread pin (or any suitable projection), but do not try this on straight stitch. This idea comes from Tecla Miceli-Schulz of Brea, California.

— Feather (Spark) Stitch —

This stitch is an extremely attractive one but is technically the hardest to do. It is not a swing needle stitch, though it may look like it at first glance. The top thread is at maximum tension and the under at minimum; a barely perceptible resistance should be felt. Since this puts considerable strain on the needle, it is more vital that the fabric for this stitch is drum tight in the hoop than for any other; any slackness will cause the needle to break. It is also necessary to hold the work down near the needle. The main effect of this stitch comes from moving the hoop in a continuous circular movement in one direction. Anticlockwise is the natural way as in writing. If you change, while stitching, to a clockwise direction you will see loose untidy stitches on the changeover. The top thread draws into a smaller arc than is made by the needle, pulling up loops of bobbin thread that make spikes on the convex curve of the line, their closeness depending on the stitch length. When it is done in straight lines you will see untidy loops that look good only if they are worked closely together making a raised texture. This is wonderful for a wall decoration, but not on garments, as it is subject to snagging. It also makes a very good filling texture worked with very small loops in one or two colours, provided your fabric will stand the strain. It is quick to do, but bear in mind that, unless the design is continuous, you may take longer finishing the ends than in doing the stitching. The top ends must be taken to the back with a hand sewing needle on the inner edge of the design (not through the needle holes or the curved line will be spoiled) and fastened with hand stitching or tying.

— Applying Shisha Mirrors —

If you can get a very pronounced stitch it can be used for sewing on shisha mirrors or large sequins. These must be stuck to the fabric, or secured with stitches across them by using the balance wheel. It is impossible to hold them. This idea comes from Debbie Casteel of Aardvark, California.

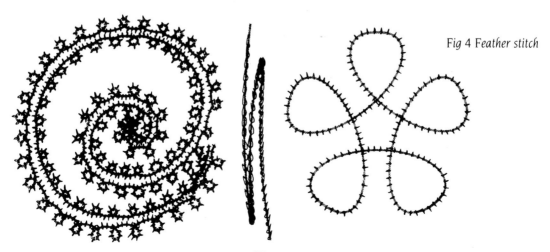

Fig 4 Feather stitch

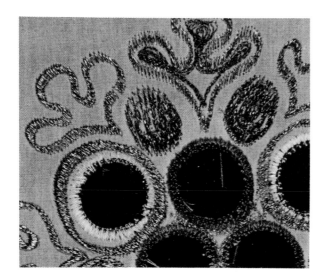

Feather and free satin stitch, 14×19.5cm (5½×7¾in). The centre sequins are held on with three stitches before feather stitching three times round the edge. The outer sequins were glued. All the other free stitching is worked with metallic thread (see colour sample on p23).

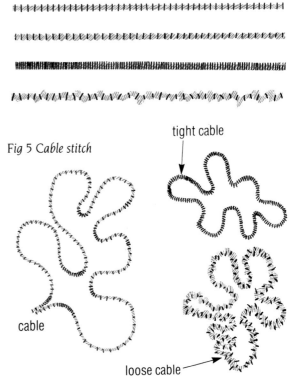

Fig 5 Cable stitch

tight cable

cable

loose cable

— Feather Stitch on Elnas ——————

The stitch is easiest to do on machines with bobbin cases. It is harder on an Elna to get the tensions as far apart as they need to be. There are two things to try if the stitch is not sufficiently spiked. Put the bobbin in the machine upside down and pass the thread through the bypass, so that it does not press against the edge of the hole, as it would normally, thereby minimising the tension. The bypass is a hole in the side of the bobbin case, normally used for heavy threads, which bypasses the tension spring. If extra tension is required on top, stand the reel on one pin and take two turns round the other pin before threading.

If you try satin stitch and presser-foot work with these settings, the bobbin coloured edges will probably be uneven and you may or may not like the effect. More regular coloured edges are obtained by loosening the top tension and working with the fabric upside down.

— Cable (Perle) Stitch ——————

Threads that are too thick to go through the needle can be wound on the bobbin. Since the effect of this stitch is on the underside, the work must be upside down in the hoop. It can be done with the presser foot or freely. It is one of the quickest, easiest and richest ways of creating texture and can be used effectively alone or to conceal the raw edges

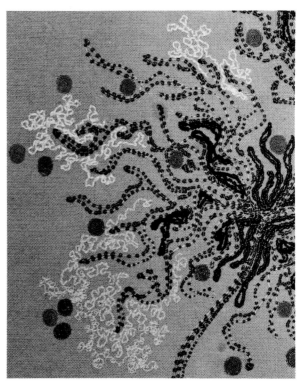

Moss cable stitch, 20.5×21.5cm (8×8½in). Loose cable worked right side up; the fabric is loosely woven, which allows loops of perle cotton to come through. The dark stitching and the white textured edges are worked wrong side up. The berries are free stitching with fine thread (see colour sample on p22).

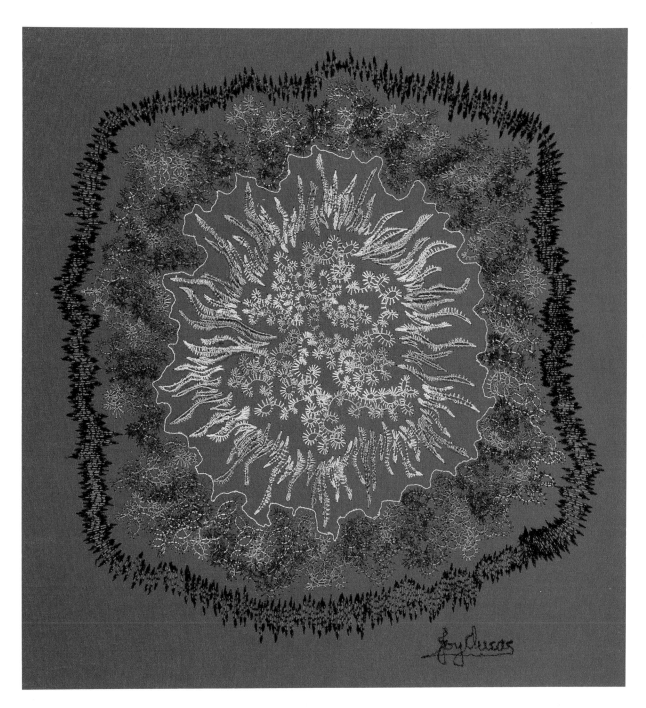

of appliqué. Used with automatic stitching, it looks very like hand embroidery. It is an excellent stitch for garments because it does not stiffen the work. Also it is better than applying threads from the top with straight stitching because with every stitch the top thread passing over the heavy one protects it.

Wind the bobbin with heavy thread by hand using thin wool, perle cotton, or any other soft yarn, though not fluffy ones that might catch on the tension spring. Use a regular thread on top and normal tension. Pull the thick thread through by

Feather stitch sample, 21×21.5cm (8¼×8½in), worked with two variegated pink threads in the bobbin; the edge was worked with black thread in the bobbin and slightly increased under tension. A deep pink sewing cotton was used in the needle throughout.

35

holding both sides of the loop, piercing a hole if it won't come through. Obviously, because the under thread is thick, it will feel tight when pulled through the tension spring. To get a normal stitch, release the bobbin tension until it feels normal. If you are not sure what 'normal' should feel like, put a bobbin of sewing thread in the machine and memorise the resistance you feel before you alter it. Always test the stitch. It should look like hand couching, but increase the top tension if you want it to look more beaded.

— Bernina Bobbin Case

Bernina bobbin cases have one screw only to hold on the spring and control the tension. If this screw is very loose, there is some danger that it will fall

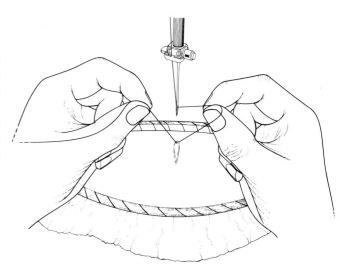

Fig 6 *How to pull up the loop of a thick bobbin thread, piercing a hole if necessary – diagram shows pulling the heavy threads to the surface in cable stitch.*

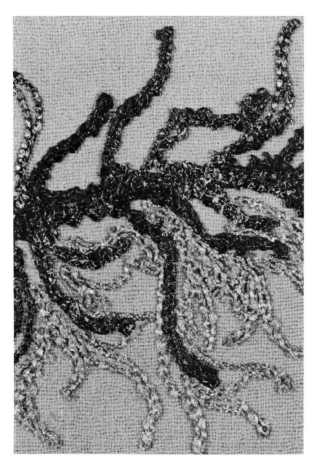

Loose cable stitch, 18.5×13.5cm (7¼×5¼in). A narrow variegated ribbon and a soft synthetic yarn were used in the bobbin (see colour sample on p19).

out. It is wise to equip yourself with a spare bobbin case, or at least a spare screw, before you start. Make sure you notice how the spring fits on just in case it falls off; the rounded end must engage in the slot in the side of the case, or the thread will break instantly. Ease the spring round until the teeth go over the edge of the space and the screw holes align. Press it very firmly against the case with thumb and left forefinger before replacing the screw. If it does not immediately engage, turn it anticlockwise first.

— Viking Bobbin Case

The Viking bobbin case has two screws; one minute one holds the tension spring on, which is nearly impossible to undo. A second, larger screw controls the tension. The old type bobbin case with a notched spring may catch thick yarn. The new type with a flap is definitely better for cable stitch.

— Elna Bypass

Elnas have a lower tension bypass (described under feather stitching), which is a special feature because it allows textured and fine slub yarns to be used. The tension of the thread against the edge of the hole is sufficient to prevent jamming. In order to thread soft yarns through this bypass, tie a knot on the end of the thread. Push it with a pin against the hole from the inside, and support it with your left index finger, pulling it through with a pin from the outside, then drop in the bobbin. Remember to cut the knot off to allow it to pass through the fabric.

Medium thickness threads can go through the spring or bypass as appropriate.

— Winding an Elna Bobbin for Cable Stitch —

For Elnas, wind the bobbin for cable stitch by hand, starting with a figure-of-eight movement so that the end is as well held as possible because it sometimes over-runs as it empties and jams the race, making it necessary to undo the last few stitches. Fill the bottom of the bobbin first and gradually work upwards. Don't be tempted to fill it too full; this prevents the thread coming out of the bobbin case from catching under a turn of the winding and jerking the bobbin upwards, causing it to snarl the top thread. This cannot happen in machines with separate bobbin cases.

— Loose Cable Stitch —

When the under tension is loosened almost to nothing, the heavy thread falls out, making an uneven line that looks like a textured yarn. This stitch is best done freely, with normal top tension. The shorter the stitch the more accentuated the effect will be. The softest yarns work best.

On an Elna it helps to emphasise the stitch if you put the bobbin in upside down so that there is no friction against the side of the bypass. This can also be helpful for automatic cable stitching.

— Moss Cable Stitch —

If loose cable stitch is worked from the right side of a very loosely woven fabric, the loops of thick thread, which normally spread sideways to form the textured line, are pulled up through the fabric to look like a fine line couched with a heavy one. For a wall hanging or panel the top thread can be carefully removed leaving the loops.

— Tight Cable Stitch —

Another cable effect involves an extremely tight under tension, and light to normal top tension. It is, in effect, a whip stitch in reverse. The bottom thread will be covered with the top, making a corded line that is much heavier than whip stitch. If the top thread is loosened further, it will begin to feather.

— Automatic Cable Stitch —

Zigzag and any automatic stitch can be combined with cable stitch resembling hand embroidery. As in

Cable and tight cable stitch, 16×16.5cm (6¼×6½in). The centres were worked with a very tight under-tension with the top loose enough to cause the stitch to feather. There is free stitching in fine thread between the white lines and outside the leaf shapes (see colour sample on p19).

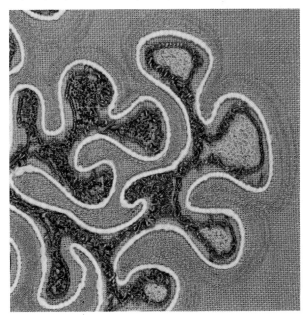

Cable and loose cable stitch, 17.5×16cm (6¾×6¼in). Loose cable follows the white line; there is fine free straight-stitching round the edge, in the loops and in the centre.

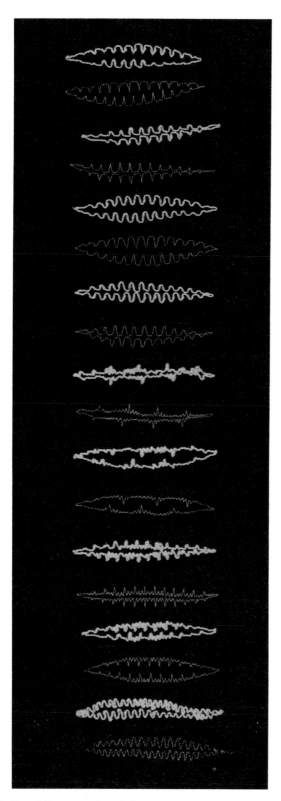

Cable with automatic stitching, 10×31cm (3½×12in). Shapes worked in pairs from the opposite sides of the cloth working in both clockwise and anticlockwise directions. If the ends on the back were to be secured under a short bar of satin stitch the work could be reversible. It was worked on firm fabric with the presser foot with no support.

Cable and automatic stitching, 14.5×37cm (5¾×14½in). Worked on an Elna air electronic using built-in stitch two, satin stitch and Disc 107 with the presser foot. Only finger pressure was used for support, but a stabiliser should be used when the work is not to be stretched (see colour sample on p19).

38

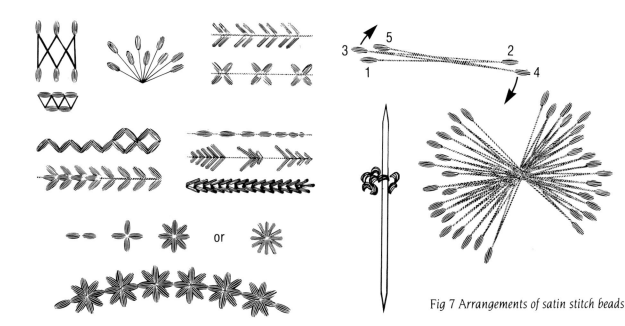

Fig 7 Arrangements of satin stitch beads

loose cable stitch there must be minimal tension on the lower thread. Stitches formed by the action of the reverse feed must be done with the presser foot or it cannot operate.

If a large area of stitching is to be done in one colour, it pays to wind several bobbins at once to minimise the irritation of changing them. All cable stitch ends should be taken through to the back with a needle.

— Satin Stitch Beads —

Satin stitch beads are most versatile stitches. You can design numerous geometric arrangements, or use them as texture, in straight lines or circles. Many of the ways of using them are illustrated here, and you will discover many more. They should be worked with the finest possible thread above and below. If a sewing cotton is used, the bulk will cause the work to get clogged and stick in the needle slot.

In describing this technique, frequent reference will be made to right and left needle position; this means the position of the needle in the cloth, not its position on the needle centring control, which should always be central.

— Working the Beads —

The beads should be built up solidly by using a short burst of full speed stitching, or have as few as four stitches, in which case work slowly enough to count them. It is only necessary to secure the threads with straight stitches underneath in the latter case. The secret of success in this stitch is the ability to hold the hoop absolutely still. Surprisingly, people find this difficult. Spread out the fingers of your left hand over the hoop and press down firmly. You need your right hand on the balance wheel. This is one of the occasions when a needle stop up is a disadvantage. It may help to remember that when there is one stitch between beads they will go in opposite directions, and when there are two, they will go in the same direction. Always keep the needle swinging, move the work

Fig 8 How to work a star accurately. For a line of stars, work a star as shown, using left swing as the centre; if the work is pivoted as shown, all the stars will be worked in the left needle position. Use a small hoop to ensure it has room to swing.

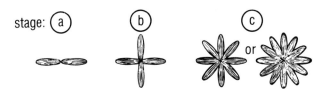

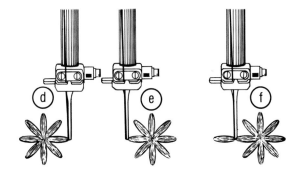

stage: (a) (b) (c) or (d) (e) (f)

Satin stitch beads, 20×20cm (8×8in). One continuous line, a satin stitch; the beads go in and out from the centre, decreasing in size at the outer edges. The stars have twelve points with only four stitches in each. The centre beads were worked over a cocktail stitch; they are surrounded by closely packed flat ones. There is free stitching between the stars and the line (see colour sample on p22).

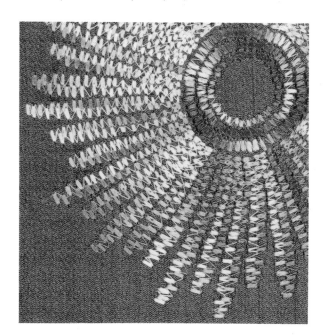

Free satin stitch beads, 18.5×18.5cm (7×7in). The machine is run continuously, moving the hoop in pauses and jerks, in and out from the centre using five variegated threads (see colour sample on p19).

beneath it to the required position, and keep your left index finger clear of the needle. Never cut the threads between beads because they become part of the design; limit their length though to 0.5cm (¼in) on a garment. Lines of beads can be tapered by making each one marginally narrower than the previous one. Width 1½ is the minimum; smaller ones chew up the fabric. The final ends should be secured by several straight stitches through the centre of the last bead.

There is no doubt that this stitch is more easily learned from a demonstration than from a book, but it is not as difficult as it appears once you have understood that the hoop must be positioned according to the needle swing. Beads need practice; but do persevere, they can be a very rewarding focal point in a design and worked in fine smooth thread they reflect light. Master a line of beads before progressing to stars.

— A *Line of Satin Stitch Beads* —

Draw a line across your practice hoop. Start at the left side with full width stitch. Work a bead, finish with a right hand stitch, raise the needle, move the hoop slightly to the left, use the balance wheel to lower the needle into the fabric, near but not touching the first bead (left stitch); the needle will now swing to the right for the next bead. Proceed until the beads are straight, evenly spaced and of uniform size.

The gap between the beads can be of any size you wish, or the beads may touch each other. An imitation of hand embroidered split stitch can be made by lowering the needle into the centre of the previous bead.

— *Satin Stitch Stars* —

This is a useful aspect of the stitch to practise next. It is sensible to use a small hoop or to be in the very middle of a large one. It is easiest if the hoop can revolve round the needle without hitting the side of the machine. The centre of the star can be in either the right or the left needle position. If you are doing a line of stars, it is convenient to use alternate positions: it saves altering the needle swing. This means that if your needle is going one way and you want it to go the other, one extra stitch, done with the balance wheel in the same hole as the last stitch, will make it go to the other side. This is necessary in some repeating stitch effects. If your hoop is too big to allow you to work a star without hitting the side of the machine, you can turn the

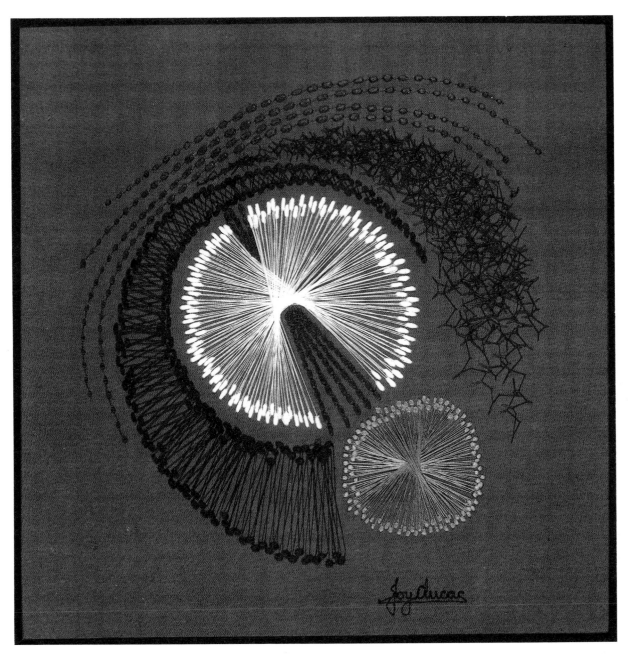

'Comet', 21.5×21.5cm (8½×8½in); *various arrangements of satin stitch beads and slow speed work with loose under-tension for the spiked textured area (see colour sample on p19).*

work through 180°, change the swing and complete the star in the other direction. (You can also do this if you are edging a hole with satin stitch.) In order to help you keep straight, do the first two opposite points on the grain (or a tack marked line), turning the work through 90°. Then stitch the cross grain beads and finally the ones in between. The centre can be either in the right or left position. If regularity is unimportant, go straight round in order. Never move the work for the next bead unless the needle is down in the centre hole. It should be at its lowest position. If the tip is only just below the edge of the needle plate, it may bend, causing the next bead to

be inaccurately placed. Inaccuracies really do spoil the whole effect.

─ A *Row of Stars* ─

If your star centre was worked in left needle position, finish on the right with the needle down on the point leading to the next star in the line. Swing the work through 90°, positioning the hoop so that the

41

Sampler with eyelets and satin stitch beads, 28×37cm (11× 14½in).

next stitch (to the left) goes into the new centre. If you have difficulty keeping straight, turn off the machine light and position a reading spot lamp beside the needle end of the machine. The shadow cast by the needle is enormously helpful. If the needle stops on the wrong side you must use the balance wheel to do the extra stitch. When you are learning it is helpful to say 'right, left, right' to yourself as you work; you must always know which way your needle is going next. If you miss a stitch, particularly when you are going from one shape to another, you will have to do an extra stitch with the balance wheel in the same spot to correct the swing. It is very easy to make a mistake. If you do, you must unpick it back to the last correct bead and secure your threads to it by more stitching on it before proceeding.

— A Circle of Beads

Satin stitch bead circles are constructed by working the beads on alternate sides of the circle. The last stitch of each bead must be on the inside. To ensure that the stitches are tight, lift the presser foot bar when crossing the circle, but lower the needle so that it is just clear of the fabric as you pull the hoop to the next bead. If the needle is too high, extra cotton will have been pulled through the needle and the long stitches may lose their tension. Provided that the beads are very closely worked, an interesting crossover of the threads in the middle will result. Work the beads in a clockwise direction. This stitch has no effect unless it is stretched.

— Bead Variations

A variation is to work the beads over a heavy needle or cocktail stick so that the beads are raised. They can be cut and straight stitched in the middle to secure them.

As in whip stitch, beads can be used as a texture by moving the hoop continuously in pauses and jerks, sideways or backwards and forwards. If a very loose under-tension is used, the beads will have bobbin coloured edges.

— Slow Speed Work

Those who have a slow speed control on their machines should use it: it enables very long stitches to be worked. Random textures worked this way are quite different from free, straight stitch or zigzag textures; they can also be varied by loosening the lower tension so that spikes of bobbin thread can

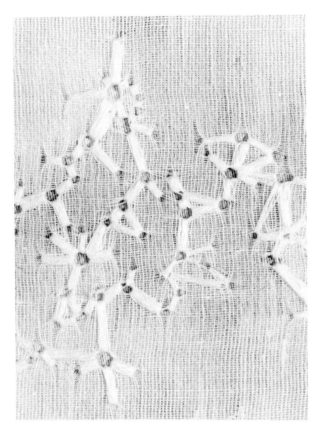

Slow speed work, 17.5×11cm (6¾×4¼in). Precise stitching building up the points, with many stitches using straight stitch and a hemstitching needle. It is mounted over a patterned fabric (see colour sample on p22).

come through to the top. As long threads catch the light, you can imagine the reflective quality of very dense stitching. It is a wonderful technique for works to be stretched; tension is necessary for maximum effect.

— Slow Speed Hemstitching

Another idea is a free development of hemstitching, where the needle travels backwards and forwards between points placed at regular or varying intervals. Work as many stitches between them as you feel makes a good effect, perhaps making some bars heavier than others. Use a hemstitch needle: it pierces a large hole that makes it easier and is more effective.

Fig 9 Precision slow speed hemstitching; this can be done with satin stitch beads, but little variation of size is possible.

— Eyelet Plates —

Eyelets are an important aspect of machine embroidery. However, eyelet plates are made only for Elnas, Vikings, Pfaffs and Berninas, the latter though is a very expensive attachment, so consider it part of the purchase price of your machine; it is worth having. Because it takes longer to fit than the others, you might as well spend a bit more and buy an extra free arm plate and have the convenience of the eyelet plate permanently set up on it. There is, though, a Viking eyelet plate costing a fraction of the amount and this can be adapted for older Berninas. It fits at the back of the feed and aligns with the needle. The front must either have the spring hooks sawn off to allow it to lie flat (in which case it must be held down with tape) or you should take the needle and eyelet plates to a metal worker to drill holes for the hooks.

Eyelets are made in different sizes; if you are buying one at a time, buy the smallest first, it allows wider stitching than the larger plate.

— Embroidering an Eyelet —

Eyelets should be worked with fine thread in a small hoop. Pierce the fabric with a sharp, narrow

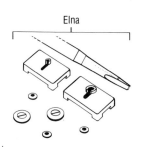

Fig 10 *Elna and Bernina eyelet plates*

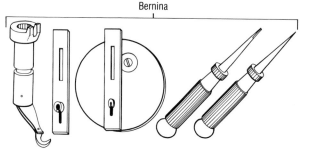

5
More
About
Stitching

instrument and be careful not to overstretch the hole (the stiletto supplied with an Elna plate is too thick). Feel through the hole for the groove down the right hand side of the eyelet plate, and press down firmly, revolving the work at the same time, which forces it down. Stitch evenly round in either direction; whichever gives the best result. To secure the thread, put stitch width to 0 and move the needle to right position over the edge of the stitching with the needle centring control, and do one or two lines of straight stitching round the edge. This is the most convenient way of finishing a single eyelet; otherwise the ends would need to be fastened on the back by hand.

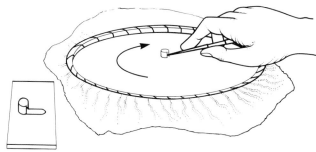

Fig 11 *How to force the fabric over an eyelet plate without stretching the fabric*

— Working Adjoining Eyelets —

Finish the first eyelet on the outside facing the next, raise the needle, lift the work whilst supporting the plate to prevent it lifting. Position work on plate as just described, work the eyelet and continue to the next eyelet position. Make sure eyelets touch or overlap, as linking threads must never be cut.

— Groups of Eyelets —

Six eyelets fit exactly round a central one of the same size. As it is hard to place them accurately, it is wise to make a template. Use a protractor to draw lines from the centre point 60° apart. The centre dots will be the width of an eyelet from the middle. Pierce the dots and mark them on the fabric with a pencil. Start with centre eyelet and work as described above.

Cut eyelets and satin stitch beads, 15.5×13cm (6×5¼in).
Both beads and eyelets are more solidly worked than usual, in
order to create a good pile effect when cut. Some eyelets are
completely cut and some partially. The cuts are supported with
straight stitch (see colour sample on p22).

Eyelets; large eyelet holes edged with the eyelet plate and satin
stitch beads, 17×17cm (6½×6½in). Satin stitch beads
are worked round holes supported with straight stitch; the dark
eyelets surrounded with straight stitching are worked on the
lower fabric. Satin stitch is worked freely; Elna pattern 5 was
used to edge the outer eyelets (see colour sample on p22).

— Alternative Stitching for Eyelets —

Eyelets need not be solid. They can be embroidered
with very few stitches giving the appearance of a
star. The more simple decorative stitches can be
used instead of satin stitch. The Pfaff is the most
exciting machine for this. It has a great range of
stitches coupled with a wide needle swing. Some of
the stitches may not go into the small eyelet plate;
finish them with a narrow satin stitch.

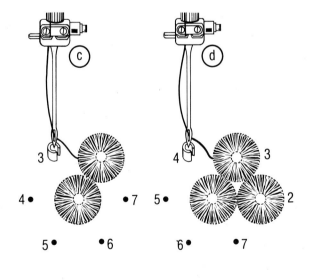

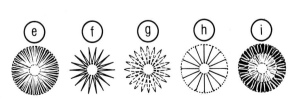

Fig 12 Alternative stitches for eyelets and the sequence for a
group of seven eyelets

45

Eyelets, 13×13cm (5×5in), worked on the Pfaff

— Eyelet Variations —

Satin stitch eyelets, if very solidly worked with the small plate, can be cut. A couple of lines of straight stitching must immediately be worked over them in order to prevent them falling out. Eyelets and satin stitch beads can be left cut or partially cut making a very rich effect; the pile is like velvet. Any cutting must be immediately supported by straight stitch. If you wish to work eyelets on a loosely woven fabric where the threads pull out of position with the swinging needle, they will be square shaped. You may like to make use of this for a decorative effect. If not, you can prevent the threads of the fabric moving by doing one or two lines of straight stitch round, with the right needle position just inside the edge of the eyelet, before working the satin stitch.

— Imitation Eyelets —

If you have a machine that does not do eyelets, there is a way to do imitation eyelets; they take longer but look just as good. Without the plate the eyelet can be any size with full width stitching, and be eliptical instead of circular.

With practice, it is possible to do free satin stitch round a small hole without the support of a plate. Until you have mastered the skill, it is easier to neaten the edge with satin stitch beads. Cut out a tiny circle, but remember that the hole will tend to

stretch. Piercing a hole is not sufficient, since you are likely to end up with a spot or star rather than with an eyelet. Start with the needle in the hole with full width left swing. Work a satin stitch bead, and make sure the needle is in the hole before repositioning the work for the next bead. For a softer effect edge, free stitch with the needle swinging and move the hoop slightly from side to side also turning it to keep the stitches at right angles to the hole. Take care not to move so far to the right that you catch the opposite side of the hole. Lock the ends with a few straight stitches. While it is not necessary to strengthen very small holes it is impossible to estimate exactly how much they will stretch. If you are embroidering a repeating border and you want the holes identical, outline them with two or three lines of free straight stitching before cutting.

— Large Eyelets —

The eyelet plate is also useful for edging larger holes, but these must be strengthened with three lines of straight stitching. Press downward with your left hand, the fingers close together so that they act as a pivot, keeping the right hand edge of the hole lightly pressed against the plate. Push the work with your right hand, helping it with a walking movement of your left fingers while you satin stitch round. To finish it, put the needle in the right hand position with centring control, straight stitch between the satin stitches by pulling the hoop slightly to the right.

— Openwork —

The ideal fabric for openwork is a very finely woven cotton. Heavier fabrics can be used, but there is more likelihood of strands of the material appearing between the satin stitched edges. Slippery fabrics such as nylon can be used, but extra care must be taken during the preparation.

Outline the shapes with three lines of straight stitching on top of one another; the stitching of any touching shapes must link or they will pull apart when cut.

When the hole is cut close to the stitching, it may fall off as the edge frays. It is essential that this vital support does not move, or the work will be distorted because the bias sections of the shapes will stretch. A looped line of straight stitch should be run round the shapes holding the edge stitching firmly to the background. Do this on a slippery fabric before you start the decorative work. You need not do it on a cotton, but if at any stage of the work you see an

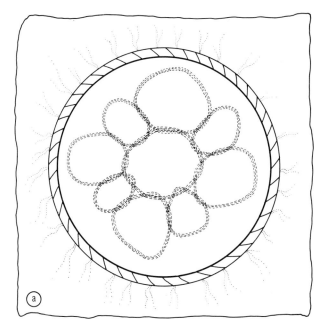

overlapping so that every shape catches onto an adjacent shape.

— Stitching Openwork —

Start with a few straight stitches along the edge to secure before crossing the hole; run the machine at a steady even speed. Beginners sometimes stitch too fast. If the threads are overtwisted they will tend to curl up and lose their tension, threads break or the machine jams; some machines, however carefully the tensions are set, make an uneven line resembling buttonholing when the hoop is moving sideways or towards you. If this happens it can be prevented by turning the hoop with every line so that you are always pushing it. This may necessitate

Fig 13 a) *The fabric in the hoop with the edges strengthened, with three lines of straight stitching all connecting with each other; they are ready to be cut out. b) The holes are strengthened with a line of straight stitching so that the support lines cannot fall off.*

edge giving way, stop and support that area before continuing.

It is important to balance your tensions before you start because the twists of the threads should be made at plate level. If the top tension is tight, they will be made up in the air pulling up bobbin thread. Not only will the resulting stitching be uneven, but there is an increased risk of the needle going down in a loop of thread and jamming. Do not use very fine thread on garments: it is too liable to damage by watch straps and jewellery.

— Openwork Shapes —

While you are learning it is wise to use round or eliptical shapes. Crescent moon or similar shapes will have unsupported inner edges. This is not the case with circles. You can have as many as you like, any size, one as large as your hoop if you wish. Either design them to be well separated or to be

Openwork, 20×28cm (8×11in), *using white top thread and deep blue in the bobbin throughout. The two small holes half way down are edged with free satin stitch, and the bottom circle is finished with satin stitch beads. Other empty circles are satin stitched, using the eyelet plate to ensure an even edge. Some holes are edged with free straight stitching, and others with zigzag, both at right angles to and parallel to the edges.*

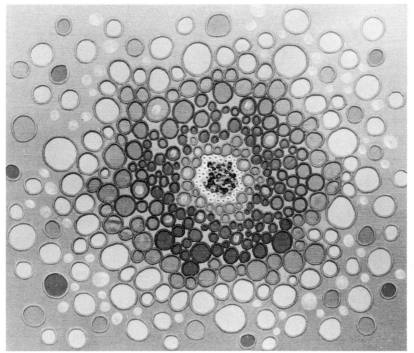

'Ionisation', 45×35cm (18×13½in) approximately. The work started from the middle after satin stitching each band of beads; the support stitching for the next band included a new fabric underneath. The top fabric was cut away so that the background colour changed with each band. A bit extravagant on fabric but great fun to do.

Experimental openwork, 14×27.5cm (5½×10¾in), with unsupported edges. Only one shape at a time must be cut and worked. The bottom layer contains slits in the fabric (see colour sample on p22).

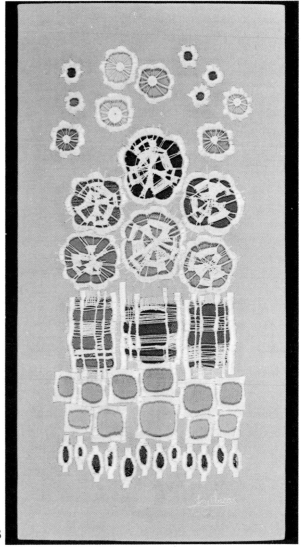

using a smaller hoop to avoid hitting the side of the machine.

Anywhere structure strands cross, solid spots can be built up from the inside, with straight stitch, by machining fairly fast. It is surprising how rarely the needle catches one of the structure lines; if it does, the space it causes can be filled up on successive rounds; finish by working towards the centre where the cut ends will not unravel or show.

Bearing in mind its purpose, the filling can be geometric or free and as solid or as delicate as you wish. Satin stitch can be used to draw strands together for a heavier look. You will get ideas from the illustrations to this chapter. If you want to include beads, sequins, curtain rings, etc, place one in front or beside the needle, use the balance wheel to step into it and again to get out of it. Stitch across the inside of a curtain ring.

— Stitching Unsupported Shapes —

If your design consists of many unsupported shapes you must cut one and stitch across it before cutting the next. If you cut them all out, the fabric will be so distorted that it will be impossible to stretch it in the hoop. Run supporting lines across the shape as soon as possible; you may find that it is easier to pull the convex edge into position if the work is not too tight in the hoop. Stitch, holding the work firmly with your fingers to prevent missed stitches. Only tighten the work when it is safe to do so after stitching. Stitching over the space following

48

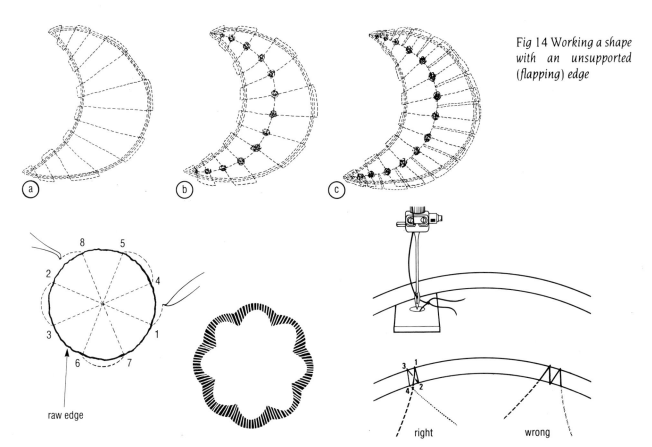

Fig 14 *Working a shape with an unsupported (flapping) edge*

a   b   c

8   5
2   4
3   1
6   7

raw edge

3 1
4 2
right   wrong

Fig 15 *Experimental openwork without supported edges; the fabric will stretch under the satin stitching.*

Fig 16 *Starting the filling for a macramé ring. Work the stitches at the edge with the balance wheel by first lying the top and bottom threads together and then working four stitches back and forth over the ring.*

the convex curve will tend to pull in towards it. It can be prevented as shown in the diagram. Having said all this, you can do it the easy way by pinning a piece of dissolving plastic under the shape, at least to get the structure lines in. The stitching may not pull in so tightly on solid circles or on satin stitching on the strands. Also there would be no curving of the threads when machining backwards or forwards over them; the work might lose something from both the technical and aesthetic point of view.

— Filling a Metal Ring —

Be sure to start with a full bobbin. Use pure cotton or good quality polyester above and below. If silver or gold is to be used, test it to make sure it does not snap. It can be difficult to tie in broken ends neatly. Put the ring under the needle, lower the eye of the needle to plate level and tie the two threads together with a reef knot. Tie it once more and trim the ends very close to the knot. Using the balance wheel, work four stitches backwards and forwards over the ring (two will not grip). Stitch steadily to the far side of the hoop. Always do four stitches over the edge, the last one going behind the

previous line of stitching; this pulls them neatly together, otherwise they would open out into a zig-zag along the metal. It is a wise precaution to do the first stitch over the last line of stitching with the balance wheel; this is the moment when the machine is most likely to tangle because the stitching is not quite flat on the machine bed.

The structure lines need not be so dense as in the gold ring illustration: the less there are the more they will curve when you stitch backwards and forwards between them. How many lines to use is a matter of commonsense and experience. Remember that you must always catch onto some stitching before changing direction or you will lose your tension and jam the race. Some interesting new ideas could be developed by putting the metal ring on a hoop with dissolving plastic in it.

— Experimental Openwork —

Rules may be broken. Openwork is one of the most interesting techniques to experiment with. So far the safe, logical ways to do it have been

described. However, one hole at a time can be cut without supporting the edges. Let the design evolve as you stitch, because you will not be sure how much the edges will give under the satin stitch. When a round hole has four equally spaced lines over it, crossing in the middle, these will act as support when the edge of the circle is satin stitched; the space between the lines will sag, making them look like petals. The raw edge can also be protected with close machine lines right across it, some of which can be satin stitched. Squares and rectangles are best cut on the grain. The background fabric can be nearly eliminated with alternate cutting and stitching.

Another idea is to cut slits on the grain and satin stitch round them without revolving the hoop. The easiest way is to use full width stitching throughout. If you have acquired the skill of moving the hoop with your left hand while the right hand operates the stitch width lever you can point them. If you want to make slits on the bias, the edges must be supported with three or four lines of straight stitch; they become quite stiff after satin stitching because the edges of the fabric roll up under the swinging needle, giving extra support to the shapes.

— Quilting —

Quilting is a very easy way to get a quick effect and it combines well with many other aspects of

50

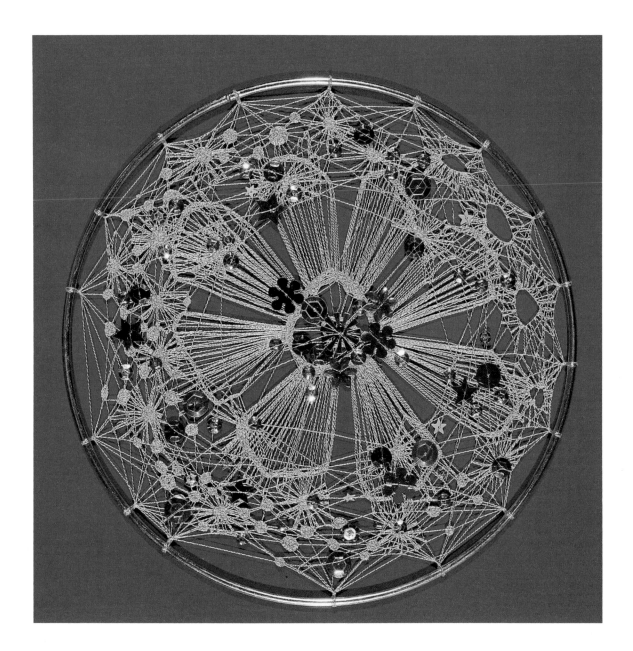

machine embroidery, especially appliqué. It can be done with the presser or walking foot, or freely. It is such a popular subject that it has been well covered in other books. However this book will not be complete without mentioning it. The quilting techniques used for hand embroidery can be imitated by machine.

— Free Quilting

Some people do free quilting successfully by stretching the work tightly in the hoop. The danger is that the thickness of the wadding (batting) may prevent the needle from getting clear of the fabric quickly enough to prevent it bending and breaking.

Openwork sample 23×23cm (9×9in). This sample shows that the fabric can almost be removed from openwork, provided that the shapes are adequately supported. The edges are all satin stitched freely. The circle is worked on the under fabric. The under fabric was pinned under the hoop and secured with the fan shaped free stitching.

Christmas decoration by Joy Clucas, 23cm (9in). The macramé ring is filled with free stitching, incorporating many sequins. Gold thread was used through the needle and yellow in the bobbin.

Quilting, 19×25.5cm (7½×10¼in). This elegant design is worked with silver thread on white fabric by Jill Harris of Flair Unique, Cairns, Australia.

In America a simple spring is sold to fit round the needle to compress the work, otherwise the darning foot will allow you to work through any thickness of wadding safely.

— English Quilting —

English quilting is worked by sandwiching a layer of wadding between two layers of fabric. For machine embroidery there will be less stiffening of the work if the lower fabric is left out and used instead as a separate lining. Precautions must be taken for preventing movement of the fabric by pinning and tacking. Refer to 'Stitching on Large Appliqué Shapes' in chapter 9 – the problem is the same.

The larger quilted shapes can be effectively contrasted with small areas of neatly drawn machine texture. An inventive person might introduce satin stitch beads, eyelets or cable stitching. The latter method is particularly good because the design can be marked on the back to prevent unwanted marks on the front of the work.

Free English quilting worked with straight stitching and a twin needle is very effective. Since it

necessitates revolving the work completely round the needle so as to keep the parallel lines apart, it is practical only for small items. Any enclosed shapes must be neatly finished by taking the ends through to the back and tying or hand finishing them.

— Trapunto Quilting —

The padding of areas or shapes in a design is called *trapunto* quilting; the top fabric should be slightly stretchy. It can be done by stitching a piece of self coloured fabric underneath or a contrasting appliqué shape on top. A small slit is made in the under fabric so that the shape can be padded with wadding or quilting wool. Do not use cotton wool, it is not soft enough. Finally, catch the cut edges of the slit together by hand.

If small appliqué shapes are loosely laid on the hoop and stitched round the edges, they will not lie flat when the hoop is removed, and the background resumes its normal tension. They are ideal for trapunto quilting.

— Italian Quilting —

Italian quilting is two parallel lines of stitching with padding between them. On some machines this can be worked on single fabric with a twin needle and appliqué foot feeding a yarn into the stitching underneath. Bernina is the easiest machine on which to do this, as it has a hole in the needle plate in front of the feed. For long lines of stitching, control the thick yarn by putting it in a saucepan on the floor. Open the bobbin access and pass the end up through the guide hole. If wished, the work may be lightly stretched in a medium sized hoop. If you try to negotiate sharp curves with this method you may find that the thick yarn misses the stitching, but if you keep some tension on the heavy thread it should stay within the needle swing. Practise on a transparent material so that you can see what is happening; increasing the top tension will accentuate the raised effect. If there is no provision for guiding heavy thread under the work, it can be wound on the bobbin.

If you cannot do this satisfactorily with the twin needle, embroider with a regular needle on a double layer of fabric. The cord can be hand tacked in position first, or fed between the fabrics from behind with a heavy needle. Bring out the needle through the under fabric and, piercing a hole if necessary, re-enter the same hole. Repeat until the whole line is padded. Test the thick yarn for shrinkage or leave an extra allowance at each end of the line.

— Drawn Thread Work —

Drawn thread work can be done easily on the machine; it can either be very free and textural, or formal, resembling hand embroidery. It can be done in bands across the fabric, or pulled at random in both directions all over the background, or contained within a shape. It blends well with openwork techniques; areas can be cut away and replaced with stitching, creating subtle changes of colour and texture. Drawn thread motifs can be cut out and used for appliqué. Braids can be embroidered and cut away from the background – particularly useful because they will lie flat round curves.

6
Advanced Techniques

control it. Alternatively pull and stitch a bit at a time. For a large work it is practical to work alternate bands and then to go back and work the bands in between, planning the colour order first. To work a block, cut carefully along a thread each side and pull the threads out from the middle. Do not throw them away as they may be useful for tassels or to be reapplied. The work should be stretched, pulling the vertical threads as tight as possible, but do not pull too tight horizontally or the cut ends will bow outwards. They should be reinforced without delay with free running zigzag in a matching colour, giving a strong edge to support any stitching that catches onto it. It can be neatened finally with satin stitching.

— Pulling Drawn Thread Work —

Most students, when learning this technique, do not thin out their fabrics nearly enough. Be prepared to spend much longer in pulling the threads out than in stitching. It is better to over- than underdo it. To help the beginner, samples were photographed before stitching.

First pull out a 4cm (1½in) band horizontally. Do not tackle a wider one because the threads have more freedom to move and become less manageable. If a wide band is wanted, leave one or two threads in the middle, or work a line of straight stitch across to

— Colour and Tension for Drawn Thread Work

The best effects for drawn thread work result from stitching with colours that blend with the fabric. A sharp contrast destroys the effect of the gently changing textures.

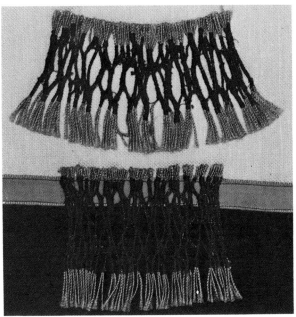

Drawn thread braid, 12×16cm, (4¾×6¼in). The braids are bands of threads pulled and worked in one direction before cutting out and reapplying with satin stitch at frequent intervals along its length.

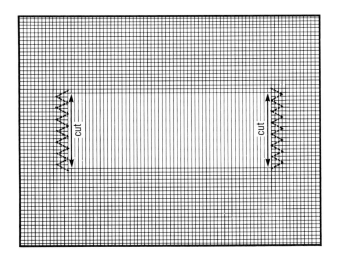

Fig 17 Preparing a block of drawn thread, one way pulling

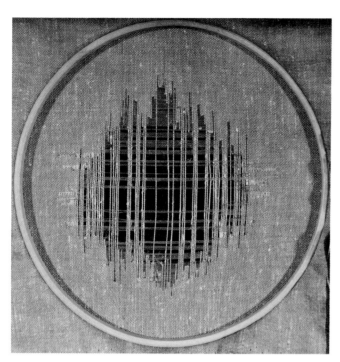

Preparation for drawn thread work

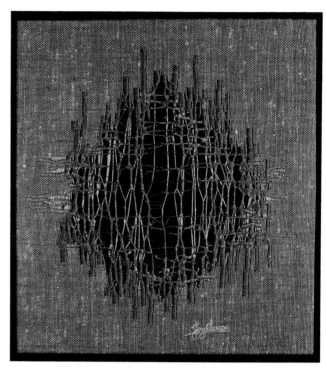

The work (of 31) completed and mounted over dark fabric 21×23cm (8¼×8in) (see colour sample on p23).

Erratic experimental pulling of threads, 28×40cm (11½× 15¾in).

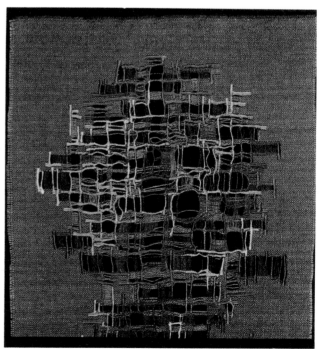

The pulled area (of 33) embroidered in a series of reds and pinks on a deep brick red ground. The piece is unfinished.

'Winter's Veil' by Joy Clucas, 40×45cm (15¾×17¾in) approximately, the experiment that turned into a panel. The veil is pulled work on butter muslin (scrim); the edges were turned in and secured with a close running zigzag, trimmed and pinned over the appliqué shapes and stitched with another line of running zigzag. This shows a quite different approach to pulled work than that shown in the detail of the scarf.

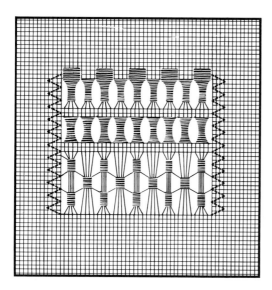

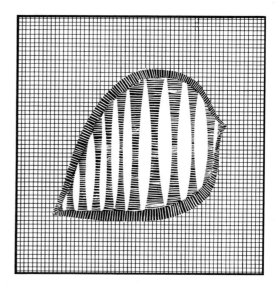

Fig 18 *Precision drawn thread work, using satin stitch over the loose threads*

Fig 19 *Contained drawn thread; the edge here is supported by stitching*

If a sharply contrasting coloured thread is used for the stitching, the restless effect can be overcome by covering all the threads with stitching, making the work very rich and solid. It is not possible to do this successfully in one go. Complete the grouping of the threads, then go backwards and forwards over the work using a slightly narrower stitch until every thread is covered.

If the work is to be seen on both sides, perfectly balanced tensions should be used, possibly using different coloured threads. Otherwise use a firm under-tension to pull the top thread to the underside.

— Stitching Drawn Thread Work —

Use full width satin stitch, which pulls groups of threads together. For the random effect shown on the curved sample, stitch up and down within the band, jerking the hoop from side to side to catch different groups of threads as you stitch. The more precise way, which looks like hand embroidery, involves more care, holding aside threads that must not get caught. You may need to stitch down and up again on the same threads to get onto the next section. If you are working bars you will need to change the needle swing with one extra stitch in the same spot for each new group. A line of satin stitch beads can also be used to group threads. If you want to include more threads in your group than will comfortably fit within your needle swing, do the first two or three stitches with the balance wheel to pull them together. Study the illustrations, they should be self explanatory. Stitching can be carried over the edges of the band as a variation.

When you work on a piece that is irregularly pulled in both directions, turn the work one way and then the other as seems appropriate. Secure every cut end under some stitching. It is hard to plan and it would be impossible to do two pieces alike. Generally speaking, if the design looks well balanced when you have removed the threads it will remain so; the pulling is the most important part.

— Contained Areas of Drawn Thread Work —

For a totally different effect, drawn thread work can be used as a filling. Outline a shape or series of shapes with three or four lines of straight stitching (extra support is needed on heavy weave fabrics). Pull out the threads within the shapes, embroider them and finish the edge with satin stitch, applied yarn or dense free stitching.

— Pulled Thread Work —

Different effects again can be discovered by satin stitching on very open plain weave fabrics, where the threads dislodge and pull tightly together within the needle swing. 'Winter's Veil' started as an experimental sampler with a number of different ideas. They need not all be on the straight grain; the red part of the stitching was done from all angles, moving the hoop in a circle round the needle. When it was finished and it seemed too good for a sampler, a lot more careful thought went into the planning of the underlay. There are many possibilities yet to be explored – perhaps they will appear in a follow-up book. You will discover many ideas for yourselves.

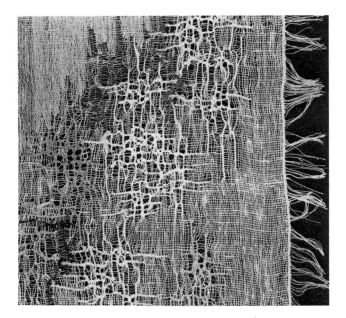

Pulled work. Part of a scrim scarf intended to be mounted over other fabrics for a wall hanging. There is an area of darning in the top left corner; 19×19cm (7½×7½in).

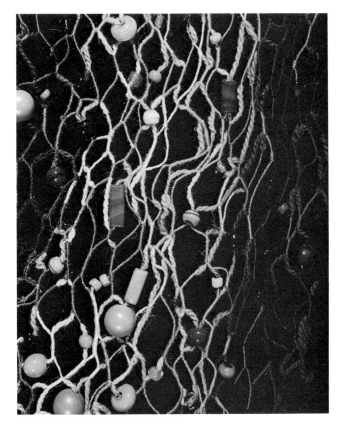

Thread wrapping, 20×25cm (8×10in). A detail of a hanging; the many coloured strands hang from a stick. To include beads, it has to be worked fom the top downwards. Parts of the yarn are uncovered to give it variety. I first learned this technique from D. J. Bennett, Lake Forest, Illinois.

— Thread Wrapping

Thread wrapping is the technique of satin stitching over a thick yarn or over three or four thinner yarns. It has many possibilities; it can be twisted and turned, and joined onto itself. The thread could be looped to break out of the stitching, tufts of yarn or fabric could be laid in front of the needle to get included into the stitching. Beads can be threaded on, new wrapped threads can be wrapped round or onto a background of wrapping, to make it three dimensional. Any size piece is possible.

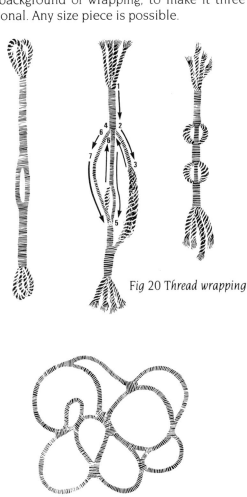

Fig 20 Thread wrapping

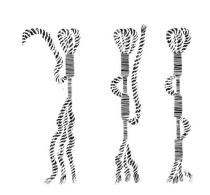

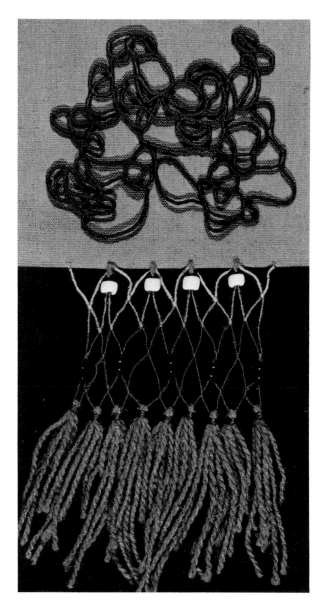

Thread wrapping, 15×30cm (6×11½in). The top part shows how a single thick yarn can be covered and bent and joined onto itself to make a firm structure. The lower part shows how finer strands can be divided and rejoined. Two extra strands of yarn were introduced for the tassels.

needle all the time, pulling behind the needle those strands that are to be left out of the stitching. This is hard to describe but is easier in practice. If a fine wire is included with the yarn, it could become three dimensional.

— Dissolving Fabrics —

As already mentioned, there are water soluble fabrics; they make all manner of open effects possible by supporting the stitching until it is sufficiently well held together to stand on its own. Lace can be made as a piece, or directly on the edge of any washable fabric, and beads and sequins can be stitched together, flower petals and other small motifs can be made for appliqué. The fabric dissolves in boiling water.

— Vanishing Muslin —

Until the dissolving fabrics came on the market, there were two ways of working open lace effects. The first was vanishing muslin, which is a brittle cotton that crumbles when ironed. It is much less practical than dissolving fabrics because many threads adhere to the work and have to be removed by hand.

— Dissolving Acetate —

Another dissolving fabric is acetate. If the embroidery is worked in pure cotton on acetate fabric, the acetate will dissolve in acetone leaving the cotton lace. It is still a useful method when some stiffness is required in the finished work. Acetone should be used in a covered glass container, as it quickly evaporates It may be necessary to give the fabric a second soaking in clean acetone; blot it dry with paper towels. Acetone is very dangerous; do not breathe the fumes and keep it well away from any source of heat. Ideally use it in the open air.

— Stitching Thread Wrapping —

The under tension should be very tight so that the top thread is pulled right round the yarn being covered. If several fine strands make the core, instead of one very heavy one, they can be divided and joined up again. When a length has been stitched, and you wish to stitch it to itself in a loop, you will need to turn the balance wheel by hand until the two parts are pulled together. You must support the yarn tightly behind and in front of the

— Dissolving Plastic —

Dissolving plastic is one of the best things that has happened in the machine embroidery world for a very long time. In fact it is pure cotton with an additional secret ingredient that makes it look like plastic. It makes many effects very much easier to achieve than hitherto. It can be used for stabilising knitwear, for monogramming or for appliqué and even to make a lace garment.

To make lace one must use the weaving principle;

Beadwork, 22×21cm (8¾×8¼in) is worked on dissolving plastic, stitched with sewing cotton for strength. It involves the use of the balance wheel most of the time; it is not quick to do, there is approximately four hours' work in this piece but it is better than doing it by hand – at least the thread is continuous. You will only be able to do this if your machine has a light balance wheel. Here the sample is mounted on the fabric with hand stitching, but it is quite strong enough for the bodice of an evening dress or the ends of a velvet or satin stole.

'Limited Spectrum 1' detail; the lace for this piece (by Pam Godderis of Calgary, Canada) was made on water soluble plastic couched onto a background of handmade paper. It stands out from the paper, producing shadows. The piece was named 'Limited Spectrum' as the fibres used in making the paper suggested the use of a particular limited spectrum of colour. The lace used straight stitch and incorporated couching and some metallic threads.

The preparation of leaves for a Christmas decoration, 23cm (9in). The leaf ends of the wires are sandwiched between two layers of organdie and satin stitched to hold them in position on the dissolving plastic. The edges of the organdie were embroidered with straight stitch, trimmed and finished, two with satin stitch and two with free texture in gold thread. In order not to waste the plastic, the remaining flowers were worked for stock. Gold thread is used on top and yellow underneath. Satin stitch beads were used in both leaves and flowers.

work two separated lines one way then backwards and forwards over them, ensuring that the needle catches every time, then work again in the first direction. Every straight line must catch onto another; every curve must be supported at frequent intervals along its length. Edges can be satin stitched for effect and support. The plastic may split behind the needle, but this will not matter. Use a fine needle and do not machine the straight stitch too fast making minute stitches; try to avoid splitting it. As a substance to work on, plastic is surprisingly strong, and it is possible to get it very tight in the hoop. Even if it does split slightly, that should not affect the tension of nearby shapes. It is possible to run some tacking lines beyond your shape to act as support, but it is not really necessary.

Plastic is nearly impossible to work on in very hot humid weather, as it sags and sticks to the user; it may even stick to itself. In a dry atmosphere dissolving plastic may become brittle; keep it in a sealed plastic bag.

— Ear-rings and Beadwork —

Dissolving plastic has made beadwork possible, which could not be done any other way. It is not possible to place a small bead on the plastic without fear of breaking it or the needle when using the foot control. The beads have to be put on by using the balance wheel. Beads in a cluster should be supported on at least three sides or they may flip over. If you miss a stitch inadvertently, you must step back to it with the balance wheel. The thread should be broken as little as possible, since it is hard to make an invisible join.

Round beads are the hardest to apply because they roll. Cast on under the bead with several stitches, hold the bead between left thumb and forefinger, raise the needle to its highest position. Put the bead under the tip of the needle while still holding it; turn the balance wheel until the bead touches the fabric, but with the needle tip just far enough down to prevent the bead rolling away, then it is easy to move the hoop under it to the correct position. Complete the stitch with the balance wheel, do a second one to step out of it, still supporting the bead with your left finger. If another bead is to be put beside the first, do at least three stitches between them to prevent thread being pulled from the machine and causing the bead to slip. Only then can you let it go. With a medium strength thread, and attention to the points just mentioned, the ear-ring should be quite robust. When rinsing out the plastic, don't do it too thoroughly, to leave a little adds crispness to the work. As it is a natural substance it is unlikely that traces left in the stitching will do any harm on a long term basis.

If beads can be sewn together, or to fabric, with the use of plastic, so can other things. Have fun – make a collection of lolly sticks, tap washers, feathers, shells, stones, etc; lay them on your hoop and see how you can join them together. This opens up a whole new field, and you could spend months experimenting.

— Freely Applied Yarn —

There are many interesting and inventive ideas that can be worked using a hoop, by laying yarn on the fabric and then stitching it down. The yarn can be curled, looped, shredded, frayed, cut into short lengths, gathered, and piled up on itself. It can even imitate hand embroidery; it can be made into tassels or tufts as you stitch. If you do not have a large supply of yarns, you can get a good selection by stripping the raw edges of coatings and tweeds. Any keen dressmaker is likely to have plenty to choose from. Muted background or softly textured areas can result from pulling out unspun sheep's wool and machining it lightly. If you have a stranded wool, pull one strand, gathering up the others on it, giving a ropelike effect with raised loops. These should be held on with stitching between the loops rather than flattening them by stitching along the length. Collect your cotton stitching ends (preferably in colour groups), arrange them on your hoop and do random stitching over them – you will get a rich textural effect. You can also use the finest silky threads from fine furnishing or dress fabrics. This could be a particularly rich technique for vests or jackets. It gives substance to the cloth without pulling it up. Yarns can also be applied with the cording foot and five-holed foot. This will be described in chapter 11.

— Stitching Applied Yarn —

The yarn can be stitched in any way that takes your fancy, such as a drawn line looping across it at intervals or with texture. The most usual way is to follow the yarn with a straight stitch down the middle of the yarn; zigzag is not suitable because it is never at the same angle as the yarn and looks untidy. The under tension should be marginally tighter than the top so that the stitching is pulled down into the yarn. If it is worked with very fine matching thread it is almost invisible. If you can

Ear-rings worked on metal frames, using plastic curtain rings, white and coloured beads and pieces of lace. The frames measure 3.5cm (1½in).

61

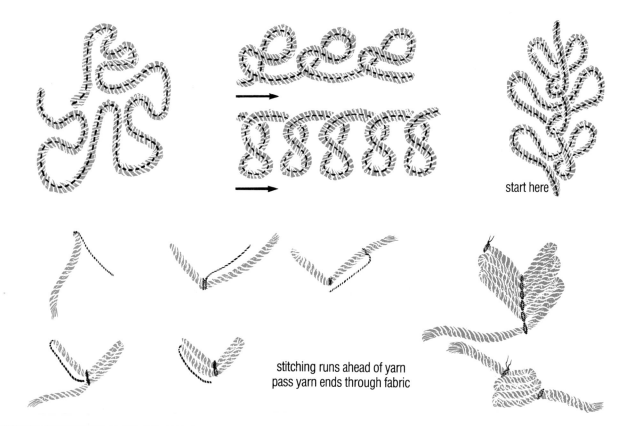

start here

stitching runs ahead of yarn
pass yarn ends through fabric

Fig 21 How to apply yarn freely for random textural effects or in order to imitate hand embroidered surface stitching, such as rosette chain stitch.

Fig 22 Showing how to catch the thread at each end of a line in imitation satin stitch and laid work. The stitching runs ahead of the needle.

'Rockcleft' by Lorna Liddell, Elgin, Scotland, 28×37cm (11×14½in). The design is taken from a sketch made in an abandoned quarry near Boat of Garten. The calico background is spray dyed and painted, then quilted to give the feeling of rocks. The ferns were made by free running stitch on vanishing muslin and, after stitching the basic shape, a fine wire was laid down the stalk and held with a fine zigzag. (Lorna says that, were she to do it again, she would choose hot water soluble fabric.) A suggestion of grass was put in by hand in straight stitch. The wired stems were pushed through the calico and anchored into the wadding behind. The finished design was placed at the back of a box frame, with an insert holding a card oval mount just behind the glass.

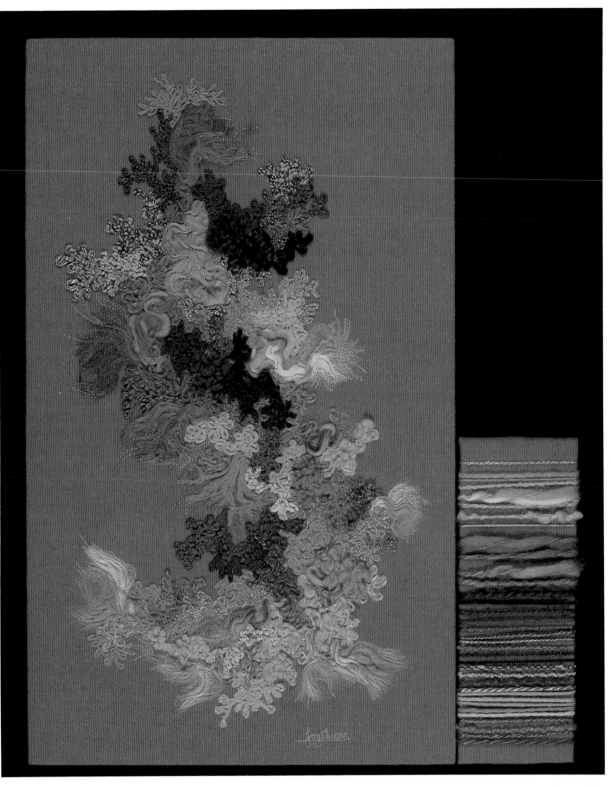

'Illumination' by Joy Clucas, 28×46cm (11×18in) has freely applied yarn. The colour sample shows that many different weights and colours of yarn were used; this is important because the design can look very flat. There are six small areas where the pile is looped, creating minor focal points.

Detail of 'Illumination', 15×20cm (6×8in), showing how yarn is applied by free stitching along it.

acquire the skill of moving the hoop with either hand while the other guides the wool, it is a fairly quick technique. At first, either pin all the yarn in position with dressmaking pins, so that both hands are free to move the hoop, or lay and stitch about 2½cm (1in) at a time. The latter, of course, means designing as you go. Start with thick yarns and with practice you will find that you can stitch a fine one. If the stitching is slipping off the yarn, stop and use the balance wheel to step on again. Imitation hand embroidery is done by laying the yarn in a repeating sequence of curves and catching it with straight stitch. For more inventive effects, satin stitch beads may be used at intervals across the yarn and to hold on tassels and tufts (see front cover).

— Cutwork Petal Shapes —

Simple cutwork can be accomplished by making slits on the grain of the fabric, and then edging them with satin stitch. If full width satin stitch is used, the slits will have blunt ends, which can make a very attractive border design. It requires considerably more skill to move the hoop with one hand and shape the stitch with the other to give the slits pointed ends. One shape at a time should be cut and stitched. If the shapes are to be done on the bias, they must be supported with two or three lines of straight stitching, and slit down the middle. The fabric will roll up under the swinging needle, giving a firm raised edge that will not stretch.

— Variety for Appliqué

Machine embroidery, broadly speaking, has two main aspects. The first, drawing with the machine, has been discussed in detail. The second is appliqué. You will immediately think of fabric shapes stitched to a background, or reverse appliqué where two or more layers of fabric are laid on top of each other. These are then cut to expose the layers underneath. There is very much more to it as you will discover as you read. It is surprising what you can attach to a piece of fabric: beads, sequins, yarns, string, pebbles, feathers, dry seaweed. The list is as long as your imagination. The machine can stitch them to a background, or to each other, with the help of the new dissolving plastic. Very original work can be done this way.

Fine, free drawing, which is the hardest part of machine embroidery, does have its limitations. It is too slow for large works and the delicate effects are not appropriate for works to be viewed from a distance. Anyone familiar with a sewing machine will not find it difficult to master the skills for perfect appliqué.

— Using the Presser Foot

While the words 'presser foot' are used throughout the appliqué chapters, it may be that you will not find the presser foot of your machine satisfactory; some feet are better than others. The problem seems to be with the shaping of the underside: some have a curved under edge behind the needle that allows the stitch to slide underneath it. Others have an angular edge that prevents the stitching from going through smoothly, the stitches pile up and the work is spoiled and must be unpicked. It may be possible to get the edge rounded off by a metal worker. Because of this problem most machine producers make an appliqué and embroidery foot, which is an optional extra. It has a groove on the underside to accommodate the bulk of the stitching. There are two reasons why it is better to use the presser foot, if possible. The first is that as it has no space between the work and the foot above the stitching, there is less chance of the fabric pulling

7
Presser Foot Work And Perfect Appliqué

up under the swinging needle. The second point is that there are no ridges underneath, so it is possible to do two curved lines of stitching side by side, without the second row catching the first or any other bulky stitching. The presser foot will ride smoothly over anything in its path. In cases of difficulty try other feet; some people like to use the open fronted foot so that they can see better – this can be an adapted presser or embroidery foot.

— Developing Appliqué

A great deal has been written about appliqué, all of which should be read. Discoveries are made by trial and error and many interesting variations of the basic method have been invented to solve particular problems. Other people's ideas can often prompt further stages of the idea and adaptations for other purposes or fabrics.

Appliqué is a very important aspect of machine embroidery. While it is possible to get bold coloured shapes by other means such as painting, spraying, batik, etc, applied fabric remains the richest and most versatile. While perhaps not so quick as the other methods, it is faster than filling a shape with free machining and will leave the fabric more supple, which is important for garments such as skirts.

— Backing the Appliqué

With appliqué, as in most subjects, experts disagree. However two things are universally acknowledged. The first is the importance of backing the cloth. This means placing some kind of support behind the work to prevent distortion. Anyone who has tried to do a curve of satin stitching without the hoop on anything but the thickest denim, will know that the closeness of satin stitch stretches the bias of a fabric and pulls thin fabrics up inside the needle swing.

The second point is the necessity of working a sample with fabrics you intend to use, not forgetting to wash, or at least test for shrinking by damping, the fabrics and pressing them until dry.

'Seed Head' by Joy Clucas, 30×30cm (12×12in). This piece consists of slits in the fabric filled with openwork or left empty, all the slits finished with free shaped satin stitch, which takes practice. The under fabric has an applied fabric shape secured with irregular free stitching. The outer leaf shapes are free straight stitching (see p64).

Leaves' by Joy Clucas, 29×25.5cm (11½×10in) uses the technique of applying yarn without stitching along it. The beginning ends are taken through the fabric. The straight stitching runs underneath the yarn, which is caught each side

of the shape. It is quite a close imitation of hand embroidery, but limited of course to straight lines. See diagrams.

(right)
Presser foot satin stitch, 15×16.5cm (6×6½in). Worked in soft colours with black bobbin thread throughout and using a slightly loose under-tension (see colour sample on p23).

(far right)
Presser foot satin stitch 15×16cm (6×6½in). The two coloured areas were worked by turning the work upside down in the hoop (see colour sample on p23).

66

— Stabilisers —

The main disagreement seems to be over the choice of backing, as it seems there are dozens to choose from. Broadly speaking there is the Vilene (pellon) range of interfacings, plain and iron on, some of which are soft and some crisp, and also the comparatively new water soluble paper and plastic. The latter has enormous potential for edging garments by creating your own lace directly onto the edge. You may even make a lace garment. It can be useful, too, for appliqué on transparent fabrics where other backings might show through or give unwanted weight, as in knits. Sometimes dissolving plastic is better placed on the front of the fabric. It can be used in combination with Tear Away (which is placed underneath) for monogramming and embroidering towels, in which case the design can be drawn on it with a permanent marker. The stiffening does not matter for small areas.

— Paper Backing —

It is not always necessary to buy these products. If none were available, most things could be done with paper. I often use wall lining paper for garment work. It is medium weight, with a rough surface that will not slide on the feed of the machine, and it is just thin enough to trace a heavily drawn design line through it. Too thin a paper is useless; if too thick, it is unmanageable under the machine and impossible to pin to the fabric. Children's cheap cartridge paper drawing books serve well, but the advantage of a roll is that any odd length or shape can be cut. You might, for instance, need to cut long strips for doing stems of flowers or a border pattern.

— Choosing the Stabiliser —

Generally speaking, the crisp commercial backings are the most satisfactory. If you find one does not serve your purpose, try another. If you are using paper, keep looking until you find the right weight rather than try to compromise by using thin paper doubled.

When deciding what method and backing to use, the most important thing to remember is that any extra layer of fabric or backing included in the stitching will stiffen it. For successful draping one layer of fabric only should be applied, which can include the addition of presser foot or free stitching when the appliqué is complete. For yokes, collars, cuffs, etc, you can incude a backing as well. You must decide what degree of stiffening is acceptable and this

is why it is so important to test your method thoroughly for each new piece of work.

— Appliqué Edges —

Appliqué is quite easy when the edges of a shape are concealed under satin stitch of uniform thickness. To shape the satin stitch to nearly nothing at the points makes the work more varied and interesting. This necessitates greater care in the preparation to ensure that the narrow areas of satin stitch are strong and neat. This is obviously more difficult than uniform width stitching, because the left hand must guide the work while the right hand operates the stitch width lever or button. This shaped satin stitching should be practised before working on your final piece, and there are two ways to do it.

Presser foot automatic cable stitching, 12×18cm (4³⁄₄× 7¹⁄₄in). Stitched with an Elna disc 150 passing the perle cotton through the bypass. The stem was worked with straight stitch without altering the tensions. The thinner lines were worked with sewing thread on top.

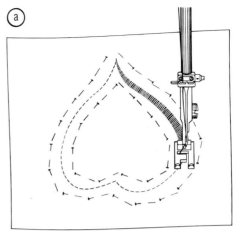

straight stitch then satin stitch shape

Presser foot automatic cable stitch using disc 107 and satin stitching. This might be an idea for a border pattern; 19×17cm (7½×6¾in) (see colour sample on p19).

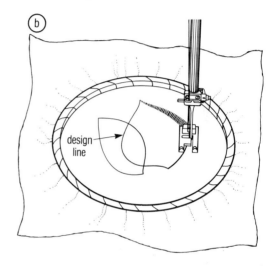

Fig 23 a) Practising presser-foot shaped satin stitching, for its own effect and in preparation for appliqué, using fabric pinned very firmly to paper. b) Presser foot work in the hoop.

— Practising Small Shapes —

For small shapes, which will fit into a 20cm (8in) or 23cm (9in) hoop, start with a simple double pointed petal or leaf shape. Draw it with a pencil, placing it well away from the edge of the hoop. Machine, starting at the point, with a close satin stitch in a clockwise direction, aiming to keep the line exactly centred under the foot. This is the easiest shape to learn on, because you will be machining comparatively straight while one hand is free to widen the stitch. Both hands will be free for negotiating the sharpest part of the curve before narrowing again two thirds of the way along.

— Practising Large Shapes —

Shapes that are too large for a hoop must be pinned to paper on both sides of the design line so that they cannot possibly move while the work is being stitched. The pinning gives you something firm to grasp. It is impossible to guide limp fabric round curves, which is why the soft stabilisers are no use.

— Right and Left Needle Position —

Remember that, when you are using the presser foot for shaped stitching, the needle on most machines can be moved into either right or left position with the needle centring lever. Whichever you choose, that side of the stitch will remain straight and the tapering will be on the other side.

— Alternative Edge Method —

This can be used as an alternative way of covering the edges of appliqué; try both ways and see which you find the easiest. Use the right hand needle position. Instead of positioning the line of straight stitching in the centre of the foot, keep it just inside the right needle position. Watch the inner edge to make sure that the straight stitch is covered as you narrow the satin stitching.

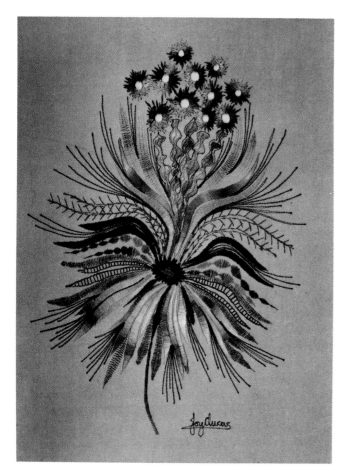

Presser foot work and imitation eyelets, 22.5×29.5cm (9×
11½in), worked on a New Home, which has a very wide satin
stitch and some interesting patterns. It has a convenient stitch
width control (see colour sample on p23).

Fig 24 Satin stitch flowers, worked with needle in left position.
These are difficult to work with needle in central position – the
hoop must be swung to try to keep the inner edge straight.

Fig 25 How to make mitred corners: machine in the direction
of the arrow; needle down at A; B and D denote outside corners
and E is an inside corner.

— Satin Stitch Flowers

The small flowers in the presser foot sampler
were worked with the needle in the left position.
Each one was a continuous line, starting from the
middle, working out and in for every petal in turn.
There is no need to mark them out unless you want
to; they are more interesting if they are slightly
irregular. The petals can be any length but, if they
are to be as short as the ones in the sample, you
should widen the stitch slowly and close it quickly
going away from the centre of the flower, and vice
versa going inwards. Not only does this make a
more interesting petal but avoids too much overlapping of stitching near the centre. Many other
interesting effects can be done this way with automatic stitches, as shown in the white flower sample,
which also illustrates cable stitch.

— Mitred Corners for Satin Stitching

The usual way to stitch round a shape is clockwise
so that any line after a corner will lie to the left
(outer corner). If you are machining a zigzag border
of full width satin stitch, alternate lines (or inside
corners) will lie to the right. First divide the corners
in half with lines of tacking thread. For the outside
corner use the right needle position for tapering the
stitch, which must be changed to left position
before the inside corner and back again afterwards.
To do this, stop before the corner with the needle in
the fabric on left swing, move the centring control to
the left. Similarly, put the needle down on the right
before bringing it back. Lower the foot and continue.
    As you approach the point, do not aim to narrow
the stitch so sharply that the inner edges of the
tapering meet on the tacking line; allow the stitches
to go slightly over it. If you work accurately coming
away from the point there will be a slight overlap of
the two lines of stitching, which will look much
better than imperfect matching.

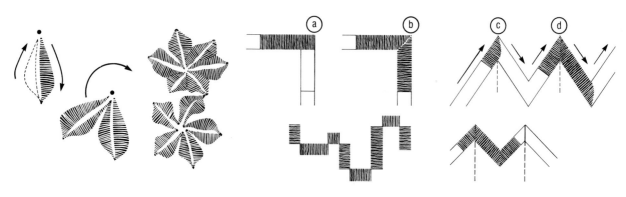

70

— Mitred Stitching on a Right Angle —

If you use the right hand needle position, there is no need to shape the stitching as you approach the corner. Turn the corner with needle down on the right, put stitch width lever to 0 and shape as you come away. To do all these corners successfully is only a matter of practice.

— An Alternative Decorative Corner —

The corners in a uniform width line of satin stitching, if always turned with the needle down on the inside, are left empty. This corner cut-out effect requires no skill and is very attractive.

— Shaped Satin Stitch on Appliqué —

When you machine an applied petal shape, rather than a practice line, you must start with straight stitching (which secures the threads), but immediately move the lever to width 1 to be sure you enclose the stitch line and the raw edge; then widen gradually. Both hands will be free to negotiate the widest part of the curve. Two thirds of the way along, your right hand must begin narrowing the stitch, as already mentioned. Reduce it to about width 1, remembering that if the stitch is too narrow the edge of the applied piece will show. Do not look at the stitch width lever; keep your eye on the stitching and judge when it is narrow enough. At

Appliqué, 22.5×22.5cm (8¾×8¾in), using paper as a stabiliser; it is embellished with automatic stitching and free straight stitching.

that point, finish with the needle down in the right hand position (outside edge). Lift the presser foot and pivot the work. If the design line is not exactly central, go back and do a few more stitches until it is. As you start machining, watch for any sign of the work sticking until the first line of stitching is clear of the foot. If it does stick, ease it through gently. As you get to the end of the second side go slowly, keeping a little stitch width. As soon as you see the first end of the stitching appear by the needle, move stitch width lever to 0 to lock the stitch. If you have a machine with more than a 4mm (¹/₁₆in) needle swing, full width may be too wide. You must decide for yourself, watching the stitch as you work. If you are negotiating a very sharp curve, the outer edge of the stitch may open out. The wider the stitch the more this will show.

— Stitch Shaping on Computer Machines —

Some computer machines need to have their stitch width buttons pressed and depressed to widen and narrow their stitches. They do not all grade down to 0. Other machines will, if you keep the finger on the widening button, widen at a set speed and decrease at the same speed on the narrowing button. Some variation in your line length can be obtained by varying the speed of the machine. The faster the machine is run, the more gradual the shaping will be and vice versa. It is not as easy as the revolving button or sliding lever and will need practice.

— Stitch Shaping on Pfaff 1222 —

The Pfaff 1222 electronic machine combines the stitch width and length in one control, so that when the stitch is widened it is also opened; there is a way of overriding it. Bring the pattern length and pattern indicator wheels to central position, depress the satin stitch petal button (shown by arrow). Set carefully the satin stitch length for the thread that you are using. The widening of the stitch is controlled on the pattern indicator wheel. Revolve it clockwise with your right forefinger, watching the stitch rather than the wheel. One revolution will open and close the stitch completely. The faster this is turned the smaller the shape will be and vice versa. If you need a very short shape, run the machine slowly and revolve the wheel quickly. Co-ordinating the revolving pattern control with the speed of the machine is not as difficult as it sounds. The other automatic stitches on this machine can also be shaped. Depress the appropriate pattern button, set all

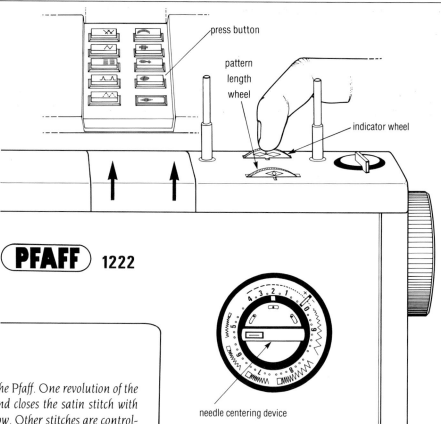

press button

pattern length wheel

indicator wheel

PFAFF 1222

needle centering device

Fig 26 *Shaping satin stitch on the Pfaff. One revolution of the pattern indicator wheel opens and closes the satin stitch with the pattern indicated by the arrow. Other stitches are controlled on the needle centering control.*

controls in central position, except for the needle centring lever, which should be on the left. The stitch will widen as this control is moved clockwise to right needle position (take care though not to go beyond it or the stitch will narrow). Turn it back again to narrow the stitch.

— Fabrics for Appliqué —

Most fabrics are suitable for appliqué in one form or another, but the method used must vary according to the thickness of the cloth. For example, it would not be appropriate to apply heavy textured furnishing fabrics with finely shaped satin stitching. The fabric used must be suitable for its purpose; for instance, delicate nylon stocking appliqué is not suitable for clothing or table linen, because it is far too easily damaged. A paper nylon, which has the same sheer quality combined with strength, should be used. Very loosely woven and open mesh fabrics are best applied to wall hangings, but they may need the extra support of free stitching on them as well as round the edges. Broadly speaking, firm, smooth, finely woven fabrics are the best choice. Pure cotton is perfect. Other natural fibres, and cotton and polyester blends are good, but they do

not yield to steam pressing as well as cotton, so your technique must be faultless. Fabrics for appliqué by satin stitching should be plain weave. A twill weave fabric is unsuitable because weft threads go over two and under one warp thread, instead of over one and under one. The strands are more likely to creep out with wear near the points of narrowed satin stitch.

— Assessment of Appliqué —

Many factors must be assessed when planning appliqué. One must consider the weight, quality and texture of both background and appliqué; whether shapes will overlap or be on top of one another as in concentric circles; the size of the work, and the size and complexity of the applied shapes. Is the pattern a one off design or is it to be repeated on the same work or at a later date? Is an item such as clothing expendable or is it to be an heirloom? Does the garment have to hang in folds or does it matter if it is stiffened with stabiliser and stitching? My method and some variations will be discussed in the next two chapters. Read everything about it; there are bound to be exceptions, so let your common sense guide you.

— Appliqué of Single Shapes to a Background

This method is suitable for any fabric, however fine and flexible. The design is transferred through to the right side from the back, stitching the appliqué piece all in one operation. The shapes should not be less than 1cm (½in) apart to allow for the extra width of the satin stitching.

If shapes of different colours are close together in the design, complete the stitching on one colour before starting on the next, as this prevents the edges of the first colour getting caught in the straight stitching of the second. Once the shape has been trimmed, it should be satin stitched without delay to prevent it fraying.

8
Perfect Appliqué With The Presser Foot

1 Draw the design on a rough surfaced paper of medium thickness, such as wall lining paper. If the design is asymmetrical, it is important to turn it over and place it against a window to transfer the design onto the back. If you neglect this, the design will be back to front on the finished work. A tracing will be needed for each repeat. A central vertical line should be drawn down each one to aid positioning.

2 Mark the positions of the motifs on the background. Fold the work in half, quarters, eighths, sixteenths, etc. If the cloth is circular, make the first fold on the straight grain. If a space calls for two motifs to be placed in it, instead of dividing the space in half, it is quite easy to do by eye. This is more practical than complicated mathematics. Crease or tack mark the folds.

3 Place the background face down on the table and lay the tracing also face down on it and secure temporarily with two pins. Use a piece of board to protect your furniture during pinning. The instructions will be given for one motif, but if you are doing a repeating design it is sensible to do them all at the same time.

4 Cut out the appliqué piece (or pieces) of fabric about 2cm (1in) larger all the way round than the finished shape, allowing for the grains to match. When a number of shapes are close together, as with the petals of a flower, use one piece of fabric large enough to encompass them all. Slide it face down under the work. To match the grains, fold the background fabric along the grain across the shape. Position the appliqué and allow the background to lie flat again.

5 Pin with points outwards (this helps to stretch the appliqué) through all three thicknesses, and across the design lines. Use pins strong enough not to bend when pushed through the stiff paper, but not glass headed ones, which get in the way of the presser foot, particularly on small shapes. Do not just scoop up the fabric. Push the pin in at an angle and bring it out against your left index finger, at approximately 1cm (½in) intervals. Finally, place pins outside any points in the design. Everything throughout the whole procedure is designed to hold the fabric rigid and support it. The fabric cannot shift between the pin going in and out; it is easier and more satisfactory than tacking. The thinner and more flexible the fabric, the closer the pins should be.

6 Turn to the right side to check that the appliqué is flat; adjust the pins if necessary.

7 Stitch with the presser foot and a normal length (2.5) straight stitch from the back along the design lines, removing the pins as you reach them. A shorter stitch might cut the paper, a longer one would not be strong enough. Because it is important to have unbroken stitching round any points for strength, start stitching in the middle of a curve where the satin stitch will be at its widest. Straight stitch is better than zigzag because it is another way of supporting the fabrics. However if very fraying, slippery fabric is to be used, a narrow zigzag over the straight stitch would give extra strength.

8 Turn the work to the right side and trim away the excess fabric very close to the stitching. If you do not cut really close, shreds of fabric may show between your satin stitching. If, instead of cutting from the edge of the appliqué fabric, you make an incision close to the stitching, the left-over piece can be used for reverse appliqué.

9 Re-pin the background fabric to the paper, placing the pins parallel to the design line and about 1.5cm (¾in) away from it, just comfortably clear of the presser foot. This is particularly

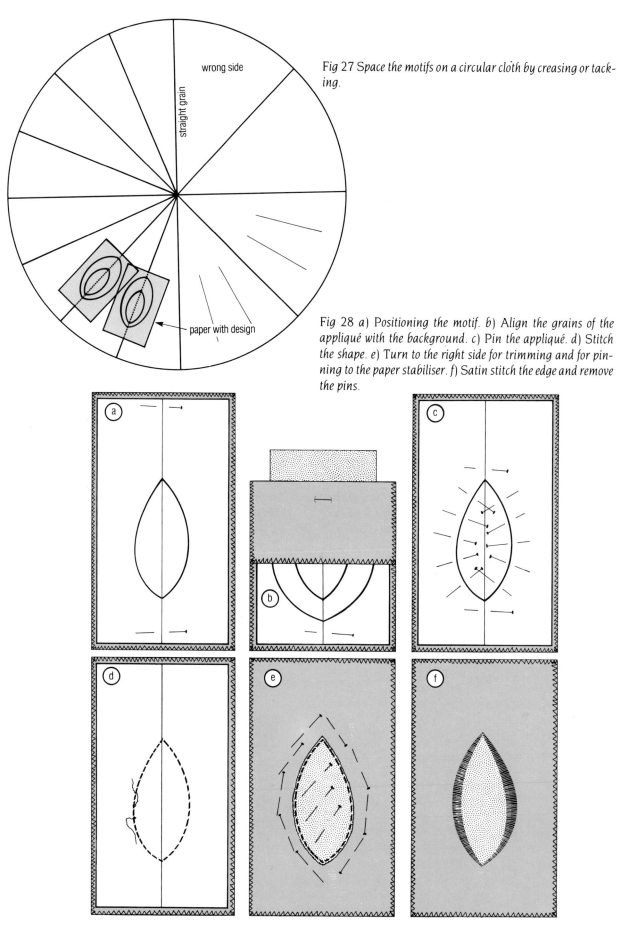

Fig 27 *Space the motifs on a circular cloth by creasing or tacking.*

wrong side

straight grain

paper with design

Fig 28 *a) Positioning the motif. b) Align the grains of the appliqué with the background. c) Pin the appliqué. d) Stitch the shape. e) Turn to the right side for trimming and for pinning to the paper stabiliser. f) Satin stitch the edge and remove the pins.*

74

important when using thin fabrics that would distort during the satin stitching. Also pin through all three thicknesses inside the design line. On very small shapes under 7.5cm (3in) long, two or three pins placed diagonally will be sufficient.

10 Satin stitch on the right side, starting at a point and shaping it as already described in the last chapter.

11 Remove the pins and paper and press. Paper will remain inside the satin stitching, but it does not appreciably stiffen the work and will become softer with washing. If the work is to be an heirloom, acid free paper should be used.

NB: never put the work in a hoop to add free embroidery until the satin stitching is completed, because the appliqué will pull out of the straight stitch as you tighten it.

— Overlapping Shapes in Different Colours —

Use the same procedure, starting with the lowest shape. The satin stitching must only go fractionally beyond the design line so that its ends are concealed in the satin stitching of the next shape.

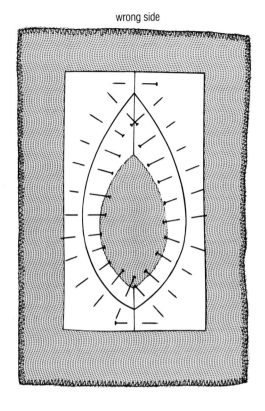

wrong side

← design line

Fig 29 *How to work overlapping shapes*

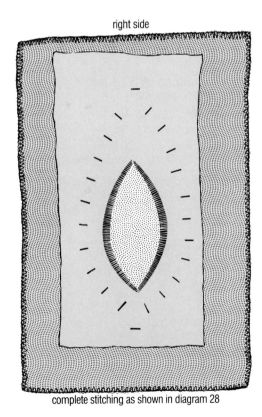

right side

complete stitching as shown in diagram 28

Fig 30 *How to appliqué concentric shapes; the first line of stitching is prepared as shown in diagram 28.*

Appliqué, 15×16cm (6×6½in); the work was stabilised in the hoop by being pinned to dissolving plastic. The leaf veins were worked in whip stitch after the appliqué was completed.

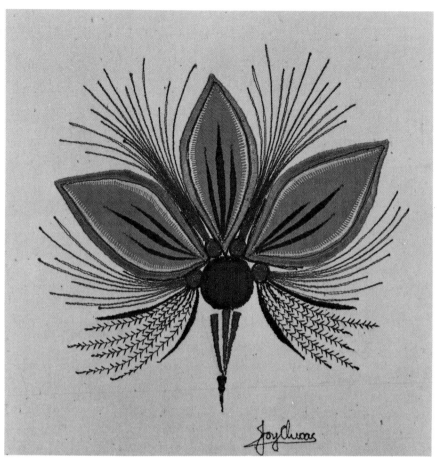

Paper is an excellent support. If, however, the design is a very large one, the paper may be unmanageable, in which case divide it into suitably sized pieces. Before you cut the paper, take a tracing of the whole design to help you reposition the sections. If the sections do not have sufficient margin for pinning, you will need to trace them onto larger pieces of paper. You must have a comfortable allowance for pinning and holding while you stitch.

— Appliqué of Concentric Shapes —

If you cut out three circles of different sizes and colours, and lay them on top of each other on a background, having stitched round the edges, the stitching of the centre circle will pass through four layers of fabric. This will impair the draping quality; also any irregularity of stitching will be transmitted to the background. These difficulties are obviated by the following method, because the stitching never passes through more than two layers of fabric. Until the outer design line is reached, you are handling only small pieces of fabric instead of the whole garment. It is not necessary to cut away any of the

under fabric (unless one wishes to), the work keeps its solidity and becomes crease resistant. Even straight stitching will prevent creasing, with or without appliqué, and it is a solution to a problem garment that has to be ironed every time it is worn.

Your first background will be the second smallest shape or circle, and the appliqué the smallest. Proceed, as already described, until the stitching of the first shape is complete. This is the point where people get confused. You do not lay the work face down and slide the next colour underneath. All that does is to hide what you have already done. Instead, you carefully lift the design paper and place it to one side, noting which is top and bottom, then lay your new fabric, the third smallest shape, face down in position over the back. It must be big enough to extend to the next design line. Replace the tracing and align the satin stitch with the edge of the hole by feeling through the fabric with the tips of your fingers. Pins passed through any points from the right side will help positioning, if the fabric is too thick to feel.

Proceed as before, until the outer design line is reached. Place the garment, or background fabric, over the appliqué. You will need to mark the position on the wrong side with tailor's tacks or pencil dots; your tracing may be useful here. Alternatively, it may be easier to lay the appliquéd pieces in position on the front surface, using sufficient pins to hold them while turning to the back to replace the tracing. Complete stitching as before.

Whenever shapes or circles are to have full width satin stitch round them, they need not be trimmed quite so closely, so that they can be finished in a hoop as in Corner Stone.

— Two Coloured Shapes —

A quick way to get an extra effect is to join two different fabrics together and press the seam open and line it up with the centre of the leaf, circle, or other simple symmetrical shape. If a number of identical shapes are to be used, as in a repeating border design, join two strips of fabric together, long enough to allow 3cm (1¼in) between each shape. If the shapes are small, up to 3cm (1¼in) wide, it is a good idea to leave wide turnings that, when pressed open, will be included in the stitching. The double layer of fabric gives the appliqué solidity. In this instance, the required direction of the seam must take precedence over the matching of grains. For this reason, only finely woven fabrics should be used when the seam will be at an angle.

— Counterchange Appliqué —

To develop this idea further, an interesting counterchange effect could be worked using pale and dark fabrics for concentric shapes. The pale fabric could be a sheer, such as organdie or nylon organza, in which case seams must be pressed to the side of the solid fabric to prevent them showing through.

In my method, just described, no fabric is cut away and so the method must be modified to get the see-through effect. Because the background fabric must be cut away after each line of satin stitching, the fabric overlap is only the width of the satin stitch, so it is vital that the stitching is extra strong.

Seam all the layers, pressing seams to the solid side, trim to 0.5cm (¼in). From the front, pin the smallest shape to the next, matching seams exactly and pinning them at frequent intervals along their lengths. Lay face down, and place design paper in position on the back. Continue as before but, in order to give the greatest possible strength, reduce the straight stitch length to 2, then go round a second time with narrow zigzag length 0.5, width 1.5. Trim the front, pin and then satin stitch. Turn to the back, discard the inner paper shape, and trim the fabric beneath it. Make a careful incision with the tip of your scissors on the transparent side next to the stitching, because you can see and prevent damage to the fabric underneath. It is essential to use extremely fine scissors; the smallest size of surgical scissors is ideal. To trim, support the fabric to be cut, and pull the scissors against the stitching for maximum closeness. Take care not to cut the turnings of the under fabric seam.

Fig 31 *The pieces left over from concentric counterchange are carefully cut off for further appliqué*

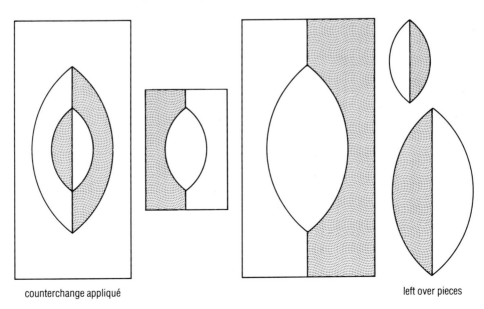

counterchange appliqué   left over pieces

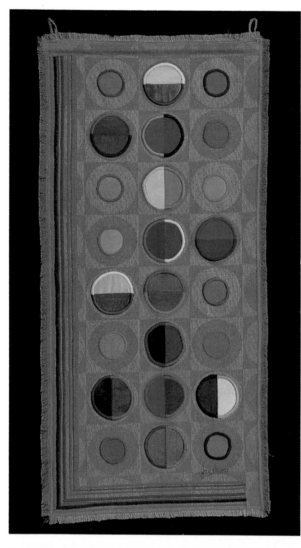

— Design With the Trimmings

If the trimming is very carefully done (cutting very close to the stitching), the pieces cut from the back can be used for appliqué and those from the front for reverse appliqué. A border design could be made, alternating the applied pieces with the excess fabric pieces. To apply these, it is sensible to use a short length running zigzag. Pin the pieces as near to the edge as possible at very frequent intervals and at right angles to it. Include some paper with thin fabrics. Machine, taking the pins out as you get to them. Run your nail along the edge to lift any loose strands, then trim with fine scissors. This makes a very neat edge that needs no further embellishment. If the edge is to be satin stitched, the regular zigzag should be used to hold it on. It can be narrower and it will cause less stiffening. It is much harder to do perfect stitching on a cut edge than on an edge that will be trimmed; meticulous care must be taken with the pinning and stitching. Further information is given in the next chapter.

— Removing the Stabiliser

When removing paper from under transparent fabrics, pull upwards and inwards towards the stitching rather than away from it. Any shreds of paper will be pulled to the centre of the stitching where they are more easily removed. Remove as many as possible, and stroke the remainder into the stitching with your nail.

It cannot be overstressed that the success of this method is in the preparation. Carefully done, it is infallible.

'Corner Stone' by Joy Clucas, 25×61cm (9¾×24in). The idea was suggested by a narrow remnant, which would have been too narrow if it had been cut to the edge of the square. A simple woven fabric such as this is a good basis for geometric design. The larger circles are seamed down the middle, giving solidity to the appliqué; the hoop was used to satin stitch the edges and paper stabilised the long lines of satin stitch.

Experimental appliqué 46×45cm (18×18in) by Joy Clucas. To make full use of counterchange appliqué with sheers, the fabric beneath must be cut away. The lower left shape was worked first. Three excess fabric shapes were cut from the front of the three stages; and three pieces from underneath. These have all been applied together with the first piece to a new background, using running zigzag.

— Appliqué With Zigzag —

While it is not possible to satin stitch round a shape to be applied without taking the precautions described in the last chapter, it is possible to zigzag round all but the sheerest and most slippery of fabrics. It is an excellent method of getting the pieces onto the background, but not the most attractive; running zigzag is preferable and, worked directly onto a cut edge, it is neat and strong.

— Appliqué With Running Zigzag —

1 Lay the applied fabrics in position, cut to size so that the grains match, unless a special effect is wanted, with stripes or to catch the light. Treat the pieces in the same way as a dress pattern; pin any points, and at frequent intervals round the edge.

2 Set a short length running zigzag, ie short enough to avoid untidy shreds of fabric showing between the points. The width can be 3 or 4 depending on the fineness of the fabric. Test it before stitching.

3 Stitch in a clockwise direction, aiming to get the right side of the stitch exactly on the edge and remove the pins as you reach them. If you are working without a stabiliser, lift the presser foot frequently to negotiate sharp curves, rather than trying to swing the work round with your hands, which might distort the fabric. This edge is much less conspicuous than normal zigzag; because the stitches are so small that they sink into the fabric, whereas the zigzag stitches catch the light. There is no risk of the work pulling up within the stitch width as in normal zigzag.

4 The action of the needle nearly always dislodges a few shreds of fabric. Run your nail along the edge in both directions, to lift the shreds, then trim with sharp fine scissors.

If you should wish to embellish the edge with satin or any other stitching, small shapes should be done in the hoop. Large shapes may be worked with a presser foot and stabiliser. Be sure to make a test piece. This stitch is extremely strong; the fabric underneath can be cut away right up to the stitching if wished. The join, even though the overlap is only the depth of the stitching, is as strong as the rest of the fabric. The only exceptions might be very fraying slippery nylon or similar fabrics. Again, test thoroughly or don't cut quite so close.

Many of us like to design as we go along. The advantage of this is that the pieces are cut to size and can be laid in position on the background fabric. You can assess, approve or alter the design as necessary, without committing yourself to any stitching. Another advantage is that you will only be stitching through two layers of fabric; turned in edges would be time consuming to do, and cause greater stiffening. Small pieces should be applied with zigzag; larger ones with running zigzag. Where two different coloured shapes overlap, catch the underlapping edge (which should be cut with a small turning) with straight stitch, just inside the line of the second shape. Only trim the turning closely if it is likely to show through. Stitching through three layers of fabric on the overlap is unavoidable. To keep the work completely flexible, the overlap of the applied pieces should be seamed, or zigzagged together, before they are placed on the background. Only you can decide if this extra work is necessary. Otherwise stitch the under shape first, starting and finishing a millimetre (about $1/32$in) beyond the second shape, so that the ends will be concealed in its stitching. Appliqué of very thick fabrics may be better dovetailed like a jigsaw than overlapped.

— Stitching on Large Appliqué Shapes —

Before stitching on a large shape (after it is applied), precautions must be taken to prevent the fabrics dislodging. Any line to be worked with the presser foot should be pinned across it at frequent intervals, including a bit of paper on the back to prevent stretching. Also pin parallel to it, on each side, so that it is well supported. Straight stitch the line removing pins on the line only before satin stitching it. If a decorative stitch is to be used, which might not hide the straight stitch, such as blind hemming or zigzag, use instead a machine tacking stitch, and remove it afterwards. Machine tacking is done with a long stitch and slightly loosened upper tension.

9
More About Appliqué And Joining Fabrics

Fig 32 *Preparing the hoop for stitching in the middle of an appliquéd shape larger than the hoop. Stitching near the edge; without careful pinning there will be movement of the fabric, making it essential to cut the under fabric to allow it to lie flat.*

Remove the lower thread first, which should pull out easily.

For free embroidery or very small presser foot shapes, press the work, lay it flat, outline the area to be embroidered with closely placed pins in a circle just inside the inner ring of your hoop. After which, the work can be stretched without fear of distortion within the pinned area. Similarly, when machining near the edge of a large shape, pin the segment of the appliqué that will lie within the hoop. Failure to prepare the work in this way will necessitate cutting the background fabric to allow the work to lie flat. This may change the colour, and the work will lose its solidity.

— Joining Fabrics —————————————

Running zigzag can be a useful way of joining pieces of fabric together to make a background.

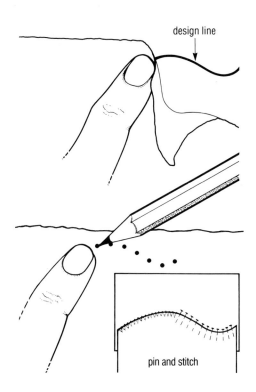

Fig 33 *Joining layers of fabric; marking the line on the cloth, cutting and pinning. Fold the fabric back to see the line, place thumbnail on the line, drop the fabric and mark with pencil. Repeat process across fabric.*

Draw the design lines on paper, mark and stitch the design in the following way:

1 Lay the second fabric with the top edge just concealing the top design line and align the fabric grain with the edge of the paper.
2 Using the left forefinger, place your nail on the design line at the right hand end. (You can see where, by lifting the fabric with your right hand.) Drop it and make a pencil dot on the fabric by the middle of your nail. Mark the whole line in this way at 2.5cm (1in) intervals.
3 Cut it, and lay it on the top fabric with grains matching. Pin frequently at right angles to edge; stitch and trim as before.
4 Turn to the back and cut away the fabric up to the stitching. Proceed downwards in this manner.

— Bias for Stained Glass Effect —————

An interesting variation of this idea is to cover the join of two coloured fabrics with bias binding or rouleau, giving a stained glass effect. Now that we can make our own with bias bars and bias makers that fold in the edges for us, the choice and quality is much wider than with commercially made binding. Instructions for bias bars are included here

1. Cut out Bias strips

Bias strip

2. Fold right sides out and machine sew ⅛″ from raw edge

Tube strip

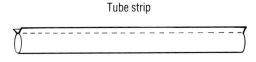

3. Insert bias bar into tube strip, bringing seam to centre of flat side

Bias bar in tube strip

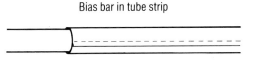

4. Steam press on both sides. Push bar through until all is pressed. You are now ready to appliqué.

Fig 34 *Making bias with bias bars*

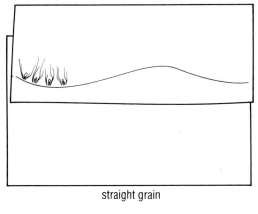

straight grain

tailor tack (double thread)

Fig 35 *Joining a curved seam by first making tailors' tacks at frequent intervals along the line of the curve. Pull apart and cut and then match the tacks carefully when pinning.*

because even though they are not widely available, a metal worker could make you some. Rouleau, and bias with turned in edges, can be applied with any stitching appropriate for the work.

— Bias Bars

Bias bars are made in America by Celtic Design Co, California, they measure ³/₁₆, ⅝ and ¾in. Cut the strips ¾, 1⅝ and 2in wide respectively. Fold in half, right sides out, then machine ⅛in from the raw edges. Insert the bias bar into the tube strip, bringing the seam to the centre of the flat side. Steam press on both sides, pushing the bar through, until the whole length is done.

— Inconspicuous Curved Seam

1 If you need to make a join with no visible stitching, you must use an open seam. To do this on a curved line, lay the two fabrics over each other with grains matching and make very neat tailor's tacks at 2.5cm (1in) intervals along the seam line, picking up the minimum amount of fabric.
2 Pin right sides together, taking care to match the tacks accurately.
3 Machine the seam, trim to 0.5cm (¼in), press the seam open and snip the curves until they lie flat.

— Appliqué for Complex Shapes

1 All the methods described so far have involved the use of the presser foot. Certain things can be done in the hoop. The presser foot is not suitable for very intricate edges. The problem with laying cut shapes on the hoop is that the background is tightly stretched, whereas the applied piece is not. When the work is taken out of the hoop, and it goes back to its normal tension, the applied piece will bubble. This can be an excellent method of quilting.
2 A motif, with a great many points, can be applied by cutting the fabric at least 2.5cm (1in) larger than the shape. Pin it very closely to the background before stretching it.
3 Another way to do it is to frame the appliqué fabric in a small hoop, and lay it on the background stretched in a larger hoop. One line of straight stitching round the edge of the shape, when cut closely, will probably pull away from the fabric; a second line, just inside the first, or a narrow zigzag over the stitching, will prevent it. It will not pull out, however, if a number of dividing design lines are machined over the shape, thus helping to support it. After straight stitching, remove all the pins (and the small hoop if used), trim closely then free satin stitch. Great care must be taken with both straight stitching and cutting, if the satin stitch is to be very narrow.

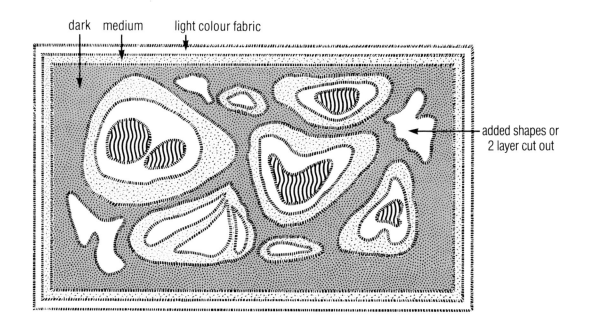

dark   medium   light colour fabric

added shapes or
2 layer cut out

Fig 37 Reverse appliqué, cutting the largest shapes first, then pinning and stitching them before adding smaller shapes in descending order of size.

Fig 36 Pinning a piece of fabric to a background so firmly that it has to stretch with the background when put in the hoop. Stitching lines on the shape support it sufficiently to allow close cutting of the intricate edge without fear of it pulling out of the stitching. If there is no supporting internal stitching, a narrow zigzag should be used over the straight stitching before trimming.

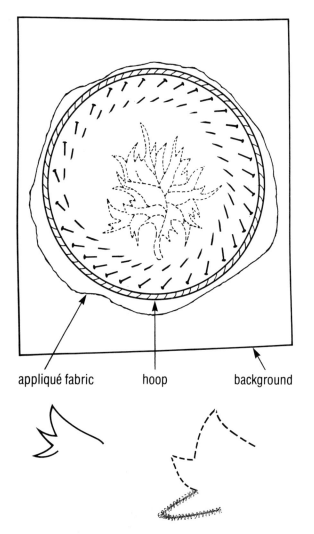

appliqué fabric   hoop   background

Fig 38 Machine tacking for small shapes of one colour

82

— Reverse Appliqué —

Reverse appliqué is comparatively easy, because the tedium of frequently matching grains is eliminated. If several layers of fabric are used, there will be no risk of the work pulling up under the satin stitching. As before, all shapes should be pinned and outlined with straight stitching before cutting. No more than two layers of fabric should be used on an article or garment that must drape. An excellent border pattern round a skirt or sleeve could be made with a wide band of fabric with interesting outlines and cut out in the middle. It could be applied with the presser foot and paper backing as described earlier. When several layers of reverse appliqué are to be used for a wall hanging, the fabrics and the straight stitching will be sufficient support, until perhaps you get to the bottom one or two layers. Start by outlining the edges of the top fabric (the largest shapes) and complete its stitching before working on the next layer. You cannot do all the stitching at the beginning, because the smaller shapes will prevent you from cutting out the big ones. If you have large holes cut away, you can also

'Summer' by Frances James, 100×66cm (39½×26½in). This is the second of four panels depicting the four seasons for a geriatric hospital. It is worked with appliqué, machine and hand embroidery, with emphasis on detail and tactile quality.

apply pieces in the spaces in the usual way, and possibly tuck other coloured pieces under some of the holes.

— Method for a Group of Small Shapes —

As an alternative method, and useful for many small shapes in one colour that would be too awkward to pin, a square of fabric can be machine tacked on the grain and cross grain at 2.5cm (1in) intervals to the background fabric, so long as they are not so loosely woven that the threads of the applied piece drag when under tension. The straight stitching can be done freely in the hoop. The tacking threads should be removed before trimming. To machine tack, use the longest straight stitch. Loosen the top tension to about half normal, and use the walking foot (if you have one) or the presser foot.

— Appliqué of Small Pieces —

So far I have discussed only zigzag and satin stitch edges, which are suitable for commercial everyday design such as clothes, cushions, table linen, etc. Sometimes, for wall hangings and special garments, softer more fluid and textural edges are appropriate. They can be finished with free stitching. Many lines of continuous straight stitch in a fine thread make a very soft edge, as does the continuous circular texture; the latter is used on the organdie leaves photographed on soluble plastic. Experimental edges may or may not be suitable for garments, and obviously techniques on wall hangings and framed embroideries can be used that cannot be used when the article has to stand up to wear and tear. It is impossible to state exactly what you should and should not do. Work samples and make your own decisions. There is a solution to every problem.

If a great number of small pieces are to be machined to a background, as in 'Flowers', they should all be laid in position, cut to size, and designed directly onto the cloth instead of onto paper. Be sure the design is well balanced before you stitch. Because, if it is wrong at this stage, it will never be corrected with subsequent stitching. Work on a polystyrene board or carpeted floor, and protect the work from children, pets and draughts. If you leave the design, it can be temporarily secured with vertical pins. If the work gets disturbed, it rarely goes back so well as the first time; it is often better to start again. Secure with safety pins, supplemented by dressmaking pins. It is not an easy task to stitch on the applied pieces in the hoop without them puckering. The simpler but long-winded way is to zigzag round the shapes. If a transparent thread is used through the needle, you will avoid frequent changing of colours. However, if there are a great many shapes, the ones left to the last may get very frayed from dragging the work continuously round the machine. On the other hand, once it is done, the straight stitching will be very much easier with the pieces already stitched.

If you tackle the design without zigzagging first, start at the right hand side and work systematically

10

More Kinds Of Appliqué

across. Spread the rest of the work out, and it will be undisturbed until stitched. Put the work in the hoop over a flower, or part of a flower, or group of shapes, moving any pins that are in the way. Generally this looks best stitched in blending colours with just an occasional sharp contrast. Study the 'Flowers'. Temporarily pin aside any overlapping shapes. Use fine thread. The difficulty is to get the applied pieces tight. Cutting them with the longest dimension on the bias makes them more flexible. The more flexible a fabric is, the easier it is to apply, but you should use only very finely woven fabrics where the grain is not visible when more than a few inches from it. Machine with straight stitch down the right side of the piece, stretching it towards you. As you go up the left side, use your nail or a mechanical device to hold the piece pulled as tightly as possible to the left. The first line of machining should not be quite on the edge. Thereafter, stitch round as many times as you find necessary to conceal the raw edge. Very slippery, or fraying fabrics, will splay out with the action of the needle; stop after a few lines to trim them before completing the stitching.

If you do not succeed in getting the piece tight, you can nick the background beneath it to allow it to give; machine it flat with two or three lines of its own colour or pad it slightly from behind. If you want to quilt it, do not attempt to pull the fabric taut. The stuffed shapes can be decorated with more stitching.

Working systematically from the right, the pinned shapes are undisturbed and cannot get damaged. After securing the petals in your hoop, work solid straight stitched petals, overlapping between each applied one. This can bring the whole design to life. The transparent effect of the overlapping stitching and fabric gives very subtle colour changes. This is an idea that does not need much knowledge of design, merely an appreciation of colour.

Very small appliqué shapes can be added to the work as you are doing it. If they are stitched over completely, they cannot bubble. For small circles, it is wise to run round the edge with straight stitch, as in the diagram. Then complete with solid stitching to conceal the raw edge. Whether you feel it necessary to hide all the edges of appliqué under stitch-

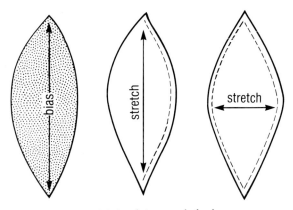

Fig 39 Applying petals freely

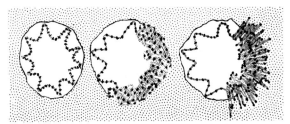

Fig 40 Applying small pieces freely

ing depends on the type of fabric and your own preferences, and the degree of strength needed for its purpose. Free textured straight stitching or automatic textures can make a change from the density of satin stitching. You will get more ideas as you read the book and experiment for yourself.

— Appliqué of Sheers —

Fine nylon stockings (pantyhose) have a lovely quality when introduced into machine embroidery, but obviously they should be used only for decorative purposes. They come in a wide range of colours and they can also be bleached and dyed. Because the shapes distort, they must be stitched and then cut. They are easy to apply and one can forget about grains. Either design as you go, or work over lightly drawn lines on the background fabric. Wonderful effects and unlimited colour combinations can be made by overlapping the shapes. Cheap nylon chiffon scarves, which are widely available, also blend well with them. Cut the stocking open and lay it on your hoop, holding it slightly stretched with your fingers or with two or three pins. Machine round the shape two or three times with straight stitch. Remove the work from the machine or trim in position, and add two or more lines of machining to conceal the raw edge. You do not need anything like so many lines round these fabrics as you do with silks, poly cottons etc.

— Shadow Appliqué —

Here is yet another idea for appliqué. Coloured shapes can be stitched underneath a transparent fabric, or be sandwiched between two layers before stitching. For the first idea, scraps of suede fabric, or any other non-fraying materials, would be ideal. Place them in position under the fabric, but pin them from the top. Put in a hoop. Design the stitching to cross the shapes to hold them flat. Small areas of the thin fabric could be cut away to show the strong colour beneath. It could also look well combined with some appliqué shapes on the top surface.

For the second idea, the under fabric could be transparent or solid. The coloured shapes could be stitched to it, and the transparent layer lightly stitched at intervals on top to hold it. If fraying fabrics are used, they must be stitched round the edge through both layers of fabric, and over them, to keep them flat. There are endless possibilities using layers of coloured transparent fabrics instead of solid ones. Coloured net is very useful here, because it remains crisp and flat when cut. Twin needle work is also very effective on transparent fabrics. Yarns, tin foil and other experimental materials could also be used.

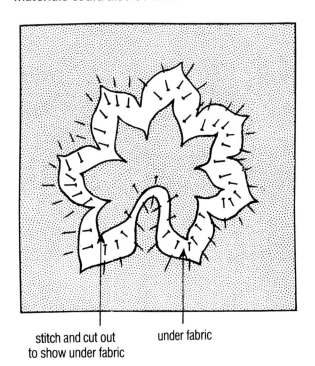

stitch and cut out   under fabric
to show under fabric

Fig 41 Shadow appliqué; stitch the applied fabric under a transparent fabric and complete both the inside and outside lines of stitching before cutting away the centre of the top fabric.

'Flowers' by Joy Clucas, 38×58cm (15×22¾in). This embroidery is so old that it is signed with her maiden name. However, after presenting American and Canadian students with a questionnaire to determine what people would like to see in the book, there were many requests for this one. In any case it is an outstanding combination of automatic stitching; this appliqué method is one that many people might like to use when soft effects are required. The background is the wrong side of white satin. Perhaps the flowers give some guidance about colour. Notice the machined petal shapes.

'Flowers' detail, 26×34cm (10½×13½in), shows the soft effect of continuous free stitching around applied shapes and the further softening of embroidered straight stitch shapes between them. Also you will see the use of several automatic stitches.

87

Appliqué and applied finished petals, 28×31.5cm (11× 12½in). Paper was used to stabilise the background for the appliqué. A large frame full of petals and leaves was prepared for a choice; they are closely worked in straight stitch with some single and some double fabric trimmed very closely and applied with free stitching.

— Applied Shapes with Pre-finished Edges —

So far I have only discussed shapes that are applied by stitching over a raw edge. Sometimes, if a very crisp effect is required, and the stiffness of extra layers of fabric does not matter, applied finished shapes can add great variety. The stitching, holding them to the background, can be on any part of them. They can be twisted, bent or bunched together, or be placed on top of each other, combined with applied ribbons or rouleau.

— Ideas for Edges —

Simple small shapes, or more complex and larger ones, can be joined with right sides together and turned inside out and the hole closed by hand. If extra stiffness is required, include an interfacing. The edge can be satin stitched, if wished, over the edge or slightly inside it. It could also be quilted. A whole garment could be constructed by overlapping these shapes using stitching to hold them together. This would be easy to do if they are pinned onto dissolving plastic and the gaps could be filled with openwork before dissolving.

For the same effect, but with less work, turn in the edges over a piece of stiff interfacing with or without the help of gathering threads, then press. You can, of course, use the old-fashioned method of hand tacking or you can zigzag or satin stitch the edge or

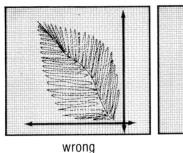 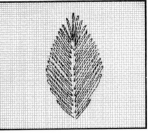

wrong   right

Fig 42 Pre-finished shapes with straight stitching, avoiding the grain to prevent it falling off

use a decorative automatic stitch and trim turnings. This will not be quite as neat on the back as the first method. It is also useful for normal appliqué when some substance is needed such as for bags, chair seats, wall hangings, etc. Shapes can be put on with a variety of stitches including straight stitch. The latter should not be too near the edge as it is all too easy to slip off the interfacing.

It is possible to turn the edges on quite small circles of fabric without pinning. Cut the circles out about 2cm (¾in) larger than you need them. Start where the grain is at right angles to the edge. Lift the foot frequently. Although you may want a narrow zigzag or satin stitch round the edge, you must use a wide one. As you turn the work you will find that if it is too narrow you will miss the fabric altogether. Do not try too hard to do a perfect circle; irregular ones are more interesting. After stitching, trim off the turning. Poly georgette is a suitable fabric; it should be uncrushable because it cannot be ironed once it is applied.

— *Edging Intricate Shapes With Satin Stitch* —

You can put fabric in a hoop; straight stitch the edge of, say, a five-heart-shaped-petal flower, then satin stitch and cut it out. This method looks unprofessional; it is very much neater if the raw edges are hidden inside the satin stitch. Put a piece of dissolving plastic in the hoop, lay a piece of fabric double, if wished for extra substance, on it. Outline

the flowers with one or two lines of straight stitching (don't use too short a stitch because you may split the plastic). Trim the excess fabric away and free satin stitch the edges. There may be splitting behind the needle, but this does not matter. It is possible to edge almost anything with the help of dissolving plastic.

Finally, shapes can be embroidered with such dense texture that the raw edges are automatically neatened when the fabric is cut a hairsbreadth from the stitching. The only thing to avoid is a straight line of stitching on the grain of the fabric – it will fall off when the shape is trimmed. Silk organza and cotton organdie are effective worked in this way. If extra stiff shapes are required, use the fabric double. Lay an extra piece of fabric on the hoop and pin it. Odd scraps can be used up, but trim the edges if they get in the way. The centres, if left with little or no embroidery, can be used to fasten the shapes to a background with free stitching eyelets or satin

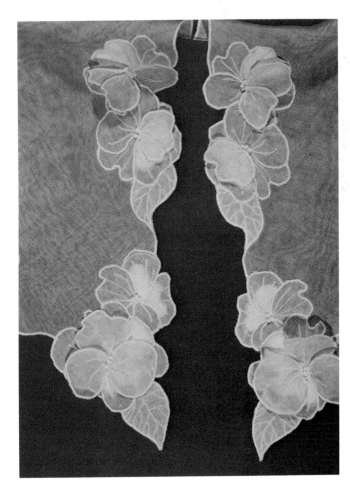

Organza collar by Jennifer Stuart showing applied and quilted flowers; some were prepared separately and applied with beads and hand stitching. It was worked with 50 DMC.

stitch beads. Spend some time preparing hoops full of shapes to give yourself an adequate selection. You may not feel like cutting them, they can look so beautiful. That is another idea.

— Suede Fabrics and Leather

The temptation to use glue is probably strongest on leather, because pins will mark it. Long narrow shapes, such as letters, can be positioned with hand tacking across but not through them; adhesive tape is probably one of the best ways, but leave it on the work for the shortest possible time. Practise the skill of supporting the work with all your fingers as you swing round curves. If a leather background is a bit

Appliqué with sheer fabrics, 23×23cm (9×9in), using nylon hose and chiffon scarves. Nylons can be used single or double, but they should be very fine. The colour combinations are unlimited. The white shadow effect can be made with paper shapes, painting or spraying through a stencil. Use an acid free paper, and the minimum of glue.

limp, secure it with hand tacking to a stabiliser under the shapes to be applied. On suede fabrics an occasional pin can be used – the marks do not show.

Experiment with edge stitches. Blind hemming stitch width 2 to 3 can be more attractive than zig-zag. Don't use too short a stitch length on leather though, you may split it. Use a leather needle.

'Country Primitive Spring' and 'Fall', each 20×12cm (8× 4¾in), worked by Ruth Maassen, St Louis Missouri, USA. The design is worked over knitting needles with satin stitch. The idea came from a cross-stitch pattern supplied by the Vanessa-Ann Collection in Ogden Utah, USA to The Needlework Times.

Decoration with beads and metal thread by Joy Clucas, 23cm (9in). The background is crystal, nylon-stitched with Madeira Astro 3. The long stitches in and out of the beads are worked turning the balance wheel by hand.

'Fish' table mats by Joy Clucas, 30.5×21.5cm (12×9in). These are two motifs from a set of twelve. They were marked out with the prick and pounce method; the heavy white lines are perle cotton applied with zigzag using the five-holed foot. The powder lines stayed long enough to complete the main lines. The designs were completed with free straight stitching.

— Presser Foot Hints —

In chapter 6 you were told how to control the stitch width lever when using the presser foot. If, instead of pointed shapes, you want to do triangular shapes ending on full needle swing, the ends must be properly fastened with straight stitch. This *can* be done beside the last satin stitch, but it does show slightly. The best way is to plan the work (its position in the hoop, etc) so that the shapes are worked from the widest end. Whether working freely or with the presser foot, reverse with straight stitch to the starting point of the shape. Swing the needle and go forward. The straight stitching will be concealed under the satin stitching.

11
Presser Foot Hints, Attachments And Accessories

— Neatening Leaf Veins —

If you wish to embroider a leaf with subsidiary veins, work the side veins first, ending centrally on the design line of the main stem. The final line of stitching will conceal the ends of the others. This is easier than tapering the stitching to merge.

— Braiding or Couching Foot —

The braiding foot is designed to guide thick yarns or cords directly under the needle. They can be held down with straight, zigzag, satin or any decorative stitch. If an item such as a cushion is going to be subjected to hard wear, it is wiser to use the running zigzag instead of the regular zigzag; it flattens the yarn and is very much stronger. It would also be sensible to use polyester thread. It is difficult to work a neat join on an enclosed shape except perhaps on a point; it is best to work in lines, or take the design off the edge. The thick thread should be passed to the back. The stitching threads should also be tied.

It may not be possible to work lines of applied yarn or cord close together, as previous lines of stitching will catch on the underside of the foot. To work a shape solidly couched with heavy thread, it is better to apply it freely in the hoop.

— Multiple Braider or Five-holed Foot —

Elna and Viking make a foot that allows up to five lengths of fine wool or embroidery thread, the thickness of no 5 perle cotton, to lie side by side under the needle. A stitch should be used that holds them separated, as they might dislodge under a zigzag. Lovely effects can be made using graded coloured strands. Hand embroidery threads are expensive, so measure off the lengths needed before threading, having tested for shrinkage. It is convenient if the design is planned to go off the edge of the work. If you have to do an enclosed shape, the beginning end or ends should be taken through the fabric with a needle before putting the foot on the machine. The finishing ends must be taken down as neatly as possible; it is difficult to disguise the join, except perhaps on a point. It is possible to work a solid shape starting from the outside using one embroidery thread through the centre hole.

— The Fringe Foot —

Most machines have a tailor tacking or fringe foot, which can be used in a very decorative way, though some are better than others. They are either too long to negotiate sharp curves, or else the bar, which loops the stitches, sticks out too far behind the needle and the stitches cannot fall off the back fast enough to embroider tight curves. The foot I use is probably an old Pfaff foot. It is not generally available but is being manufactured again in America. It is an ideal foot because it is short in length and has two bars to raise the stitching so that two rows of smaller tufts can be made by using a twin needle. The next best thing is the Elna fringe foot; it needs the back end of the central bar sawn off to facilitate very curved stitching. Depending on the complexity of the design, the work may have to be done in a fairly small hoop. Crisp cotton, or polyester or heavy rayon thread should be used, 50 machine embroidery cotton is too soft and lacks the essential substance. This technique is not suitable for garments, as it is too easily snagged. The stitching can be cut but it should be supported with a line of straight stitching down the middle.

stage 1   stage 2

Fig 43 *The easy way to merge satin stitch lines. Begin a triangle of satin stitching by reversing to the wide end.*

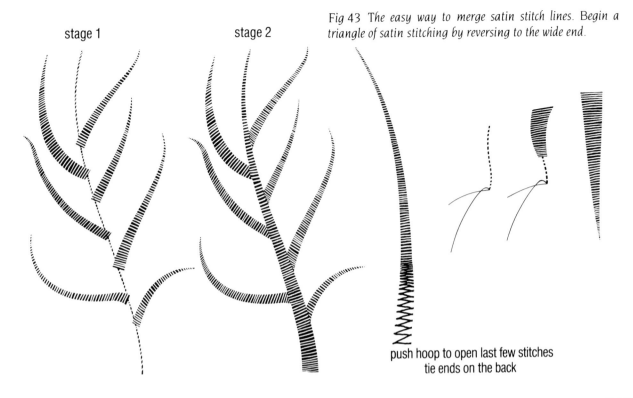

push hoop to open last few stitches
tie ends on the back

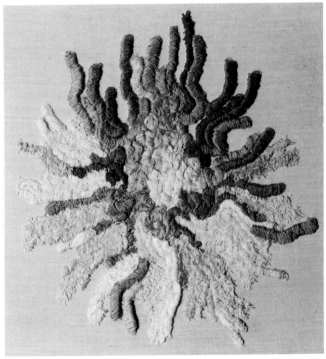

Thread applied with the cording foot, 18.5×19.5cm (7¼× 7¾in). Yarns of varying thicknesses and textures are applied with zigzag. The four lines in the centre were applied using the central hole of the five-holed foot. The white inside them was applied freely, which demonstrates well the difference between the two methods (see colour sample on p19).

Embroidery with the fringe foot, 23.5×24cm (9¼×9½in). This must be one of the richest textures of all, but it is not every fringe foot that allows such tight curves to be worked. The pile is partially cut. The work is not signed – it will be extended one day (see colour sample on p22).

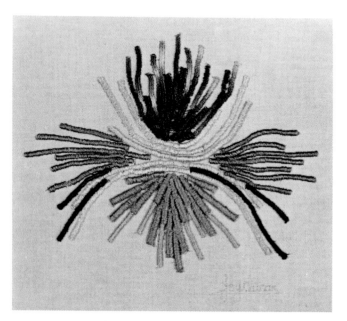

Experimental raised work, 17.5×15cm (7×6in). This was an effort to use the knitting needle technique in a creative way. It is worked with Natesh thread, using cocktail sticks, plastic string and nylon cord to raise the stitching (see colour sample on p23).

Attachments

While machines have their own attachments, some are interchangeable. There is a fitting called an adaptor for Berninas. The lower end has a screw that will allow Elna, Viking or most Pfaff feet to be used, though not slant needle machine feet. In the last few years this has been made more complicated by clip-on feet. Both the shank and the clip-on foot must be transferred. Clip-on feet have been known to cause imperfect stitching. The shank is best removed for free embroidery because it may catch on any raised stitching.

Attachments for Decorative Work

The other most useful attachments are the eyelet plates. Their use has been described fully in chapter 5. There are also various other mechanical aids for decorative work and monogramming. Find out which ones can be used for your machine; refer to accessory lists. Remember that some may interchange. Every machine has its own special features, but, since this book is mostly concerned with creative stitching, only the most useful ones for combining with free embroidery will be mentioned here.

Circular Sewing Bar

Bernina and Elna manufacture a bar that clips onto the machine to enable perfect circles of automatic stitching to be accomplished. At the end of the bar a pin holds the fabric and the work rotates round it. The work must be very well stabilised underneath the fabric with paper, or must be stretched very tightly in the hoop. You may improvise with a drawing pin taped upside down to the machine; it also helps to put some masking tape under the middle of the fabric, which will prevent the threads from being pulled out of position while machining, thus ensuring greater accuracy. The slight compressing or elongating of an automatic stitch that may be necessary to complete the circle perfectly takes practice.

Accessories

Accessories such as the knitting needles, the Elna rug fork and the Viking weaver's reed can be used with any machine.

Knitting Needle Work

A very interesting technique has been developed in America of satin stitching over fine steel knitting needles, which gives a very rich raised pile. In America sets of needles are sold for this work, but any needle that fits within the needle swing will do. The work is stabilised by ironing freezer paper on to the back. It is not very practical to do it in the hoop, as it would be necessary to use much shorter needles. Semicircular needles are used in addition to straight ones.

Experimental Raised Satin Stitch

To make much freer use of this technique, try stitching over other things such as cocktail sticks, bodkins, heavy cord or plastic string. Do not stitch too long a length at a time or you may not be able to remove the core.

The Elna Rug Fork

Rugs can be made by winding yarn tightly round the fork and stitching up the middle directly onto the fabric, making two rows of loops, which can be left whole or cut. It is only possible to work in straight lines across the hessian (burlap). There are greater decorative possibilities if the fork is used to make a fringe, which can be applied to the fabric,

'Summer Flowers', 15.5×23cm (6×9in); eyelets and presser foot work (see colour sample on p19).

then it can be curved or looped and held down with applied yarn or any other effect that might seem appropriate. For a much smaller fringe, hairpin lace frames can be used, or even a piece of bent wire coathanger.

— The Viking Weaver's Reed —

The Viking weaver's reed is also used for making rugs, but it works rather differently. The Elna fork has a raised end, allowing wool to be wound on as it is needed to stitch over any length of fabric, whereas the weaver's reed has a channel for the stitching down one side so that it is dual purpose. When the groove is on the right hand side, the pile will form to the left for making rugs. When it is turned over and the stitching is on the left side, it is used for making and stitching a fringe onto an edge in one action. As with the Elna fork, the fringe can be made separately.

— Fabric Marking Aids —

There are dozens of books on hand embroidery, but comparatively few on machine embroidery. The methods for marking out designs are the same for both. Since they have been well documented, they will be listed here only briefly.

It is a good rule to have as little marking on the front of the work as possible; this is important for machine embroidery where fine drawing and open textures may not conceal the lines.

There are many aids for marking the fabric, some of which disappear with time or with washing but you may find, in a few years, that the fabric beneath them disappears as well! These aids are sometimes corrosive chemicals, so except for expendable items, be on the safe side and do not use them; stay with old-fashioned methods.

— Prick and Pounce —

The prick and pounce method is a very good one for machine embroidery. The design can be perforated easily on greaseproof or tracing paper by machining with a fine needle, freely or with the presser foot. The design is transferred to the fabric by rubbing black or white pounce powder through the holes with a soft pad and then painting over the holes with poster colour. For machine embroidery the painting may not be necessary. Unless the work is a very large one, the powder lines will stay long enough to embroider sufficient of the design to be able to complete it freehand. If the powder disappears, it is easy to lay the tracing on again and rub more powder through it.

If presser foot cable stitch is to be used for the basis of a design, it can be pounced on the back from the reverse side of the tracing, or if the background is thin, the tracing can be used as a stabiliser.

— Machining Design Lines —

For a very structured design, it is expedient to pin the tracing to the fabric, above or below (if it is needed as a stabiliser), and machine the main lines, which could then be incorporated into the design.

12
Transferring The Design; Finishing; Care Of Work

Use the presser foot, if it is a large motif, or work freely in the hoop if it is a small one, using a straight stitch so that the paper tears away cleanly. Dissolving plastic can be substituted for the tracing, but it is essential to use an indelible marker so that it cannot stain the fabric when dissolved. It can remain throughout the embroidery, helping to support fabric such as terry towelling (it also controls the pile). However, this method is expensive for a large piece. Knitted fabrics should include a stabiliser underneath; a fine lawn will cause the minimum stiffening otherwise Stitch and Tear or Tear Away can be used. Pull away the edges of the dissolving plastic; small bits left in the stitching can be sprayed with water, allowed to dry and removed with a brush. All traces will be removed with washing.

— Pencil, Tailor's Chalk and Tacking —

Pencil on light coloured fabrics and tailor's chalk on dark fabrics can be used with discretion. If you decide that they are appropriate, you may be able to trace the design directly onto the cloth. Strengthen the design lines on the tracing paper with a felt pen, tape it to a window with the fabric in position over it and transfer the design.

A geometric design of straight lines could be marked out with pencil dots and a ruler; you should be able to stitch straight between dots up to 7cm (3in) apart. The lead will shine on a dark fabric. If you think it is worth the trouble you can hand tack the lines. They certainly leave no trace but there is some likelihood that they may get caught in the stitching. It really depends on how precise or accurate the stitching needs to be. The whole business is really a matter of common sense.

— Stencils and Templates —

A stencil made with light card could be convenient for repeating small simple designs on both the background and the appliqué piece and facilitate matching the grains accurately. Templates may also be useful.

Fine quilting poses a problem; any marking on the front surface is likely to show. This is a strong case for designing as you go. If you cannot, you may have to resort to the old-fashioned methods of pinning and tacking. It is no wonder that everyone welcomed the wash-away markers. As there have been some sad accidents after their use on quilts, be safe rather than sorry; do not use them. Paper or dissolving plastic could carry the design for small pieces, but it is too expensive and cumbersome on large ones. Do not trace with pencil as it would soil the thread.

— Finishing the Work

You have not finished when the embroidery is complete. Work is often let down by poor presentation. One can pass the work on to the appropriate experts, but it is cheaper and better to learn to do it oneself.

— Edging a Sheer Fabric

It is not the purpose of this book to discuss dressmaking techniques. You will find many ideas for decorative edges for fabric in your machine manuals. There are, however, two methods that are worth mentioning because they are particularly useful for the embroiderer. The first method is excellent for silk and poly georgette. You may find it in your instruction book but it conveniently omits to tell you how to turn a corner. The second method is an extremely fast way of edging strips of cloth neatly, which could be used for appliqué, and which might be an interesting combination with applied fabric and yarn.

— Shell Edging

1   Cut the fabric to be edged on the grain with a normal seam allowance. Thread the machine with matching 50 machine embroidery cotton or fine rayon thread.
2   With wrong side up, turn in the seam allowance on the left side and put in a pin to hold it while you start to machine.
3   Use blind hemming stitch, stitch length approximately .75, width 2. Still wrong side up, place the left side of the work under the needle, so that the bulk of the work is between the needle and the side of the machine. Position it so that left needle swing goes over the edge.
4   Stitch the edge, turning in the seam allowance as you go, supporting the work in front of and behind the needle. Stop before the end.
5   Snip the fabric in front of the needle, at right angles to the edge on the fold line of the next side. Allow it to spring open. Continue stitching to the snip.
6   With the needle in the fabric, preferably just after two sideways stitches, lift the presser foot, turn the work to the next edge, fold in the seam allowance and, using a pin, bring the cut flap round to the right side of the needle and lower the presser foot.
7   Continue stitching, helping the fabric to feed through with the tip of a pin if necessary until it is completely under the presser foot.
8   Continue on round until you are nearly at the beginning. Cut away a short length of the first turning so that the fabric is not doubled in the stitching near the corner.

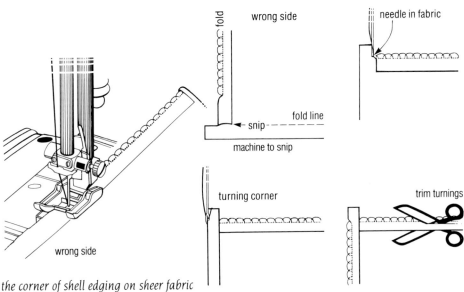

Fig 44 Turning the corner of shell edging on sheer fabric

9 Lock threads with a few extra straight stitches. Trim turnings very close to the stitching and press.

— Shell Edging on a Bias Edge —

If a shell edge must be done on a bias edge, it must be supported before stitching. Run a matching machine gathering line using small stitches along the edge, just inside the fold. Pull it up to the correct tension and tie the ends. Stitch as described above.

— Edging Silk Chiffon —

Some fabrics, such as silk chiffon, are too fine to support shell edge stitching, in which case you will find that it works well with a narrow zigzag instead.

— Zigzag Edge With the Buttonhole Foot —

This edge is very much quicker than the last edge because the edge of the fabric is rolled into the stitching by the grooves on the underside of the foot, so that the trimming process is eliminated. It does however necessitate very neat cutting, and it must be stitched before it frays. It is debatable whether it is quicker to do this, or to tear the fabric and use the first method. For a quality finish, the first method is recommended.

'Plettenberg Bay' by Joy Clucas, 69.5×35.5cm (27½× 14in), was worked with a wide variety of machine embroidery and sewing threads using free, straight, zigzag stitch and satin stitch beads.

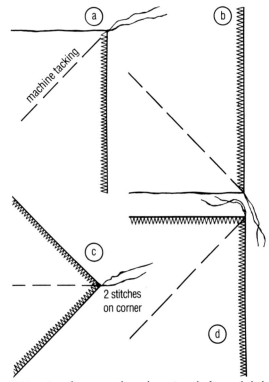

Fig 45 Turning the corner of an edge using the buttonhole foot

Detail of 'Plettenberg Bay'. This is a good example of very varied texture using free zigzag, circular fine stitching and satin stitch beads. The foam is in many shades of white, pale green and blue.

98

1 Prepare the corners with a diagonal line of machine tacking in each, dividing them in half. Leave long ends on the corners.
2 Use the buttonhole foot to stitch length 1.5 to 2, stitch width 3.
3 Line up the right edge of the work with the inner edge of the right side of the presser foot. Start stitching on the corner diagonal tacking, with the work right side up; use the tacking ends to support the work and to help it to move, until the presser foot grips the fabric evenly.
4 Stitch until the needle touches the next diagonal with the left swing.
5 Raise the foot and turn the work through 45° and do two stitches on the corner with the balance wheel.
6 Turn to the new line of stitching and continue round in the same way. Help with the tacking threads if necessary.

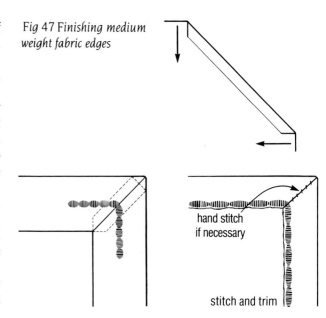

Fig 47 Finishing medium weight fabric edges

hand stitch if necessary

stitch and trim

— Medium Weight Edges —

For edges suitable for table mats, etc, where greater strength is needed, a single fold should be turned in mitring the corners. Any decorative stitch can be used to secure the fold. Finally, trim the turnings up to the stitching. On a bias hem tack the turning with paper or stabiliser over it, turn to the right side, do two lines of straight stitching round with sewing cotton for strength before changing to a finer thread to work a decorative stitch over it. Tear away the paper, trim the turning and press.

Where it is not necessary to turn corners, as for sleeve and skirt hems, you will find other ideas in dressmaking books and your machine manuals.

There are many books to tell you how to make cushions and curtains, cover boxes, make handbags, etc. Refer to them if you have problems.

— Stretching a Panel —

Work can be done on fabric that is to be framed and stretched that obviously would not be possible on garments. Even if your work is so encrusted with stitching that it wrinkles, it will almost certainly be coaxed flat by the following method.
1 Steam press, getting someone to help you pull it into shape as you do it.
2 The edges must be strengthened. Buy enough bias binding (the coarse variety is best) to go

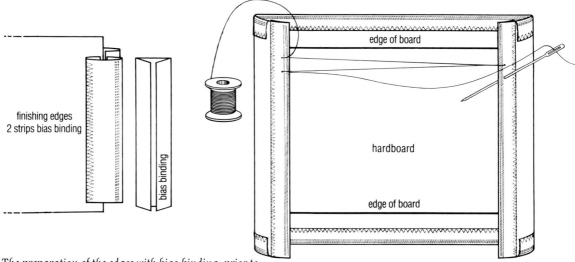

finishing edges 2 strips bias binding

bias binding

edge of board

hardboard

edge of board

Fig 46 The preparation of the edges with bias binding, prior to stretching. Lace the work behind the bars of straight stitch.

twice round the edge of your work. Sandwich each edge between two pieces of binding right sides out, but only half over the fabric. It is important that the background fabric is not included in the outer straight stitching. This is because the bias acts as a shock absorber to prevent the distortion marks from tightening the string being transmitted to the front of the work. Never lace into the fabric itself.

3 Stitch through the two layers of binding and the edge of the fabric with running zigzag at full width, feeding the binding under the foot as you go. For fraying fabrics, stitch round a second time catching the edge of the binding onto the background.

4 Hold the outer edges of the binding together with two or three lines of straight stitch. This forms a strong bar to support the lacing. Without it, the bias binding would tear.

5 Lace with a large needle and fine twine behind a straight stitching line. Use strong button thread, fish line, etc, preferably not rayon twine, which will curl and twist as you work. Stand the reel of thread in a saucepan on the floor. Lace right across a small work, the longest dimension first; or half at a time for a large one.

6 Straighten the work, secure the needle end with two half hitches (buttonhole stitches), and tighten the string back onto the reel to avoid waste. Cut and secure temporarily by winding round a pin.

7 Lace the other half and keep stretching the edges outwards along the board as you tighten the strings.

8 It may be necessary to tighten the string several times. Ease the fabric from the front with the palms of your hands until it lies perfectly straight along the edge. To help judge if you have tightened it enough, pull the other edges firmly outwards. Fasten the end and stretch the other sides in the same way. Do not mitre the corners. It weakens the fabric and may show.

— *Stretching Fabrics on Macramé Rings*—

For small gifts, and Christmas and wall decorations, you can stretch fabric onto a metal ring. It can be done before or after the embroidery.

1 Cut the fabric 2.5cm (1in) larger all the way round than the ring. Run two machine gathering lines round the edge, using strong polyester thread (slip top tension and pull up the work with the bobbin thread).

2 Draw the edges in over the ring and pull the

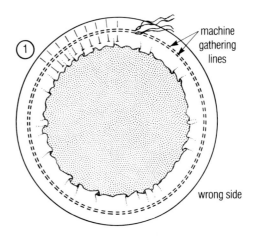

stretching fabric over a macrame ring

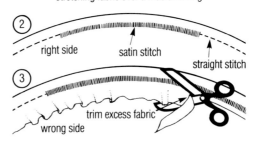

Fig 48 *Stretching fabric over a macramé ring with gathering threads or pins, or both. Work a straight stitch then a narrow satin stitch. Trim.*

threads as tight as possible and tie them together.

3 If this has not succeeded in getting the work really tight, use pins at right angles to the edge on the grain first, then cross grain and between at about 2.5cm (1in) intervals. The larger the ring, the harder it is to get the gathering threads tight. If you prefer, you can do it entirely with pins, but using more of them.

4 Stitch with a zip foot able to move to either side of the needle; put it in the left position and do a line of straight stitching very close to the edge, followed by a line of satin stitching, which will give it a final tightening. Trim the raw edge.

— *Stretching on Square Metal Frames* —

Stretching on a square metal frame (obtainable in America) is done in a similar way, pinning the sides first. Gathering threads that are run round the corners will help them to lie flat. Another idea is to cover the wire with bias binding before stitching. Make a neat crossway join, hand tack the edges together inside the ring. This will greatly speed up the embroidery; only one stitch onto the binding is needed instead of four stitches over the wire. When the stitching is finished, the tacking can be removed, the edges will be held in the stitching.

— Finishing Wall Hangings —

There are various ways of finishing edges and hanging a wall hanging. The simplest and quite effective way is to use an automatic stitch about 1cm (½in) from the edges and then to fray them. Where there is a central motif there is very likely to be some pulling up of the work, which means that there will be a slight bagginess in the edges. If it is very slight, it may be taken up in the top and bottom hems; if not, run a hand or machine gathering line down the sides to absorb the fullness evenly. Stitch a narrow tape or ribbon on the back to hold it rigid. Very few hangings drape perfectly, because of the uneven weight of fabric and thread. Lining a wall hanging may make the back of it look neater and will help to prolong its life, but on the whole it adds to the problems; it is one more element to contend with. A hanging with lining or heavy appliqué should never be rolled; it will get badly distorted and it is more difficult to press once it is lined.

If you have managed to stretch work successfully, you may like to progress to simple framing. The two most difficult aspects of framing for the layman are the cutting of the mount and the moulding. The chances are you will not need a mount, or you will extend your embroidery by screwing the stretched work onto a larger fabric covered board. Most framing shops will sell you moulding cut to your measurements. All you need is a Stanley frame clamp, woodwork adhesive, light card for backing, a lightweight hammer and panel pins, and gum strip or tape for neatening the back.

The frame clamp consists of four plastic corners with a string passing through the outside grooves, which must be tightened until the clamp is bar taut. Modern adhesives are so good that further strengthening is not necessary. If the frame is handled roughly it is better that it should fall apart than it should split. If you are likely to do frames often, it is worth investing in a Red Devil stapler, which more than halves the time spent in fitting the frames. Panel pins are not too difficult to manage provided you have a really small hammer. Include a lightweight card to hide the strings, and neaten with gum strip or adhesive tape.

— Care of Textiles —

This is a good moment to say something about the care of textiles. The main hazards are light, dirt, insects and acid from paper and wood. For conservation purposes use only acid free paper. Hardboard is suitable for stretching textiles. Karen Finch recommends a layer of linen under the work, but that means that her method of stretching should be used. Her book *Caring for Textiles* should be read by all textile artists, both for care and conservation and for methods of stretching and hanging work. (See also *The Care and Presentation of Textiles* by Karen Finch and Greta Putnam.)

We should all do what we can to lengthen the life of any textile that we make, and work on the proviso that prevention is better than cure. Fabrics should be stored in acid free boxes ideally but, at the very least, cardboard boxes should be lined with acid free paper or with well washed cotton fabric. They should be stored in the dark, in an even cool temperature. For non-washable textiles, take particular care to keep your hands clean. Acid can emanate from your skin.

Fabric is a tactile substance, a quality that is partially lost when the material is placed under glass, but in the long term, this is the best way. The work should be mounted just clear of the glass, and the whole frame should be sealed to protect it from dust.

Karen Finch recommends vacuuming hangings through nylon filament screening (filtration fabric) held just clear of the work. As this is not widely available you can improvise with a piece of fine nylon net stretched in a hoop. Clean both sides of a hanging. In some instances a gentle shaking will do no harm. Avoid brushing, which may damage the surface. If there is no other way of getting into crevices, use a fine sable paintbrush. If, in the course of working, you get a bad stain necessitating a cleaning fluid, the whole thing should be dry cleaned or washed. Always remove oil based stains first, then water stains. When dry cleaning, protect the surface by tacking nylon net all over it and encase the whole work in a calico bag and tack it again. When in doubt seek the advice of a conservator. Mistakes can be irrevocable.

We would all like to be able to create our own designs. It is possible to do so whether we have any art experience or not. Everyone has some imagination and since there is inspiration all around us, designing might be described as the amalgamation of the two.

13
Design
And
Colour

— Learning to See —

If you attend a design class, you will be encouraged to look and see. Many people are not fully aware of the infinite variety of pattern, colour and texture around us. If we learn to look at things with a more developed perception, not only will our lives be enriched by the pleasure we derive from it, but ideas will get stored in the best computers in the world – our brains.

Photographers understand this very well as their lives are a search for symmetry of line, form and colour. They may find it in the shadows through railings, the curl of a leaf, or in the structure of buildings. To study their work is a good way to learn.

The more we see, the more we learn. Recognising these things, whether or not we record them with a sketch book or camera, will influence us indirectly.

— Balance of the Design —

There are many elements in a good design: shape, balance, colour, tone values, and texture. The painter or photographer has only to concern himself with the space within his frame, whereas the craftsperson must design not only the decoration, but the item itself, or at least blend the two. Designs on a garment should harmonise with its shape.

You might think that there should be a set of rules such as, balance a coloured shape on one side of the work, with two smaller ones in a similar colour on the other side. It may be that you will want to do this, but the whole business is intuitive rather than mechanical.

— Geometric Design —

Geometric design is much harder than might be imagined. A weakness in the structure of a design may go almost unnoticed in a rich mass of colour and texture, but not in a simple structure of circles and squares. The balance has to be perfect. In many ways it is more satisfying than free work and it can be vibrant, with simple shapes in rich colours.

— The Focal Points —

A design may consist of lines or shapes, or a combination of the two; remember that the spaces between the shapes are an integral part of the design, and will be more interesting if the sizes vary. It is likely that the largest shape placed somewhere near, but not exactly in, the middle will make the main focal point (except perhaps in geometric design or symmetrical design). There may be other focal points, but they will be subordinate to it. Careful thought should be given to the placing of the focal areas. A focal point can be something other than a large shape. It may be some rich texture or an extra strong colour area. In a flower, the lines of the petals converge to a colourful centre. Nature is one of the greatest tutors of design and colour, if we take the time to look at and record it.

— Lines in the Design —

There should also be variety in the thickness, lengths and angles of your lines. Groups of lines should vary in size, density and direction. Curves should not be merely a segment of a circle, they should sharpen and fade out and change direction.

Equal amounts of anything, whether it is two colours, textures or lines, are rarely harmonious. One colour group should predominate, texture should be set off with a smaller or larger plain area. The spaces in a design should vary in size and shape, the shapes themselves must vary. A student learning to draw is taught to vary pencil pressure and so tail off a line. It is the same with machine embroidery.

Many embroideries have been spoiled by stalks being added to flowers as an afterthought. If a design must have them, they should be considered at an early stage, almost before the flowers; they are an important part of the structure and rhythm. Groups of leaves or machine texture could be used to pull a design together instead, or it may even be better left alone. Watch other art forms for good stalk structures. Memorise and record them.

'Low Tide', 25.5×27.5cm (10×11in). If inspiration does not come to you, try working on a bold printed fabric or a lightly textured one. This is worked with whip and straight stitch (see colour sample on p23).

— Diagonal Lines

Similarly, sets of diagonals are hard for the beginner to design. You will find them in many places; cracks in a pavement or glass, or stalks in a cornfield. Or, more practically, find a photo of a tree in winter. Cut large squares out of one corner of two sheets of paper and use the resulting L-shaped pieces as an adjustable frame to search within the photo for a balanced structure. This way extraneous detail can be eliminated. It may be that even a small area will provide you with a varied and graceful set of lines. You may find fifty or more ideas in the one photo, and this is a very good way to discover something original. Often a part is more interesting than the whole; it might lead to a very exciting appliqué.

— Texture

Texture is an important component of a design. It may be used to enhance smooth areas and to give enrichment for focal areas. You have learned many ways of creating it in preceding chapters.

— Colour

There have been some good books written about colour, and these the creative embroiderer should read. There is room here only to make some practical suggestions to help you to make your work more varied.

It does not matter whether a design is bold or muted; each can be good in its own context. A design can be worked in one colour, but it will be more dependent on the other factors already discussed than a many-coloured scheme. Subtle variations will play an important part. Designs using one colour group are comparatively easy. The old adage 'blue and green should never be seen' is really not true. Today we use colours that our grandparents

'Eye of the Storm', 53×44cm (21¾×17¼in), is worked in white, cream, dull greens and copper. Originally the central motif was meant to be on its own, but a mark on the fabric that could not be disguised led to the work being expanded.

105

would say 'clashed', and this can give great excitement to a colour scheme. It is safe, but dull, to use a range of similar blues, ranging from very pale blue to navy; bring in a few touches of a greeny blue and the design will have more life and vitality. It's exactly the same with quiet colours; bring a touch of mauve pink to a range of peaches. The operative word being 'a touch'; equal quantities of 'clashing' colours do just that. This point is illustrated in the appliqué skirt. It has small touches of bright green and blue.

It is more difficult to plan a work with many colours. They must not be mixed up indiscriminately. Each colour group should be seen almost as a design on its own and be balanced, however sparse, then they will be good in combination. The sharp colours will probably be the last you will position, giving emphasis where it is needed. This emphasis may be echoed more softly in the stitching of an appliqué.

Above all, do not be afraid of colour. There are no written rules and ultimately it is what pleases you that matters. Use brilliant green and orange, reds and blues together. Remember that bright colours can be enhanced with the dull greens and mauves, and that strong colours do not necessarily need a subdued background. Tone values are a part of colour, as seen in a black and white photo. The greater the tone contrast, the more dramatic the work will be. To help assess the tone values of a work, half shut your eyes to cloud the colour. If the colours seem right, the tone values take care of themselves.

If you feel that colour is your weak point, help yourself with frequent trips to your local art gallery and library. Play with colour. Cut a square of every colour you can find from old magazines. Use them to help you with your work; try overlapping them to help you assess proportions. In most areas it is possible to attend classes in design and colour, but most important of all learn 'to see'.

— Finding Inspiration —————————

Some people are born with design sense; others have to learn it. If you are unsure of yourself, facing

'Late Summer Evening' by Sylvia Naylor, Bedford. The calico background is tinted with Procion dyes using an air brush. The embroidery is mostly whip stitch, with hand embroidered long stitches and French knots.

a blank piece of paper or an empty hoop is very inhibiting. We cannot all be artists, but we can all learn to borrow ideas and they are all around us. Look at your dishes, curtains, jewellery, children's books, pot plants and your garden. To go a little further, the machine embroideress should look at wedding gowns and embroidered fabrics; some are exquisite and the ideas can always be adapted for the domestic machine. The techniques are basically the same. Studying commercially embroidered textiles will help you to decide which techniques will blend. While you are learning, it is a good rule to avoid bringing too many ideas into one piece of work. The result may look confused; this point is quite well illustrated in my work. The variety that is so important is provided more by vibrant colour and rich texture than by a hotchpotch of stitching techniques. This is not to say that they should never be mixed, but it must be done with discretion.

Designing is fun, and there are ways to do it that do not involve drawing and painting. Whether it is an adaptation of some other art form, a natural object, or your own imagination, you can give the idea a tangible form with the very special effects of fabric and thread.

'Evening Bloom' by Joy Clucas, 80×60cm (31½×15½in) approximately. Worked from a pencil sketch directly onto the fabric with appliqué, satin and free stitching.

— When is it Finished? —

Assessing your own work is difficult and the hardest moment of all is deciding when you have finished. If there is time, it helps to put it away and come back to it with a fresh eye. If there is not, help yourself by looking at it from far enough away to obscure the detail. This is a great help in assessing balance; also look at it upside down, or in a mirror, or buy a reducing glass.

If you have read this far you will have appreciated how many ways there are to vary the mechanical stitch. The words 'machine embroidery' tend to create the wrong impression, but the English language, usually so prolific, does not provide a neat alternative. It is our control over that needle that matters. Recognising that something does not look right is the first stage of design awareness. How to put it right is harder to learn and the points listed in the next chapter may help you.

— Buying the Fabric

Choosing a material for any given project is a matter of common sense, and there is plenty of choice. Be sure to choose one suitable for the stitch techniques that you plan to use, and buy sufficient extra fabric to test your ideas, both from the design and technical points of view. Plan your colour scheme with available fabrics rather than trying to find colours for some preconceived idea. Since the eye can distinguish at least three thousand shades of colour you are unlikely to be able to find an exact shade.

14
Creating Your Design

— How to Draw

There are a number of ways in which you may like to design and these will depend on your skill, design awareness and personality. If you feel confident enough to draw with, or without, a source of inspiration, do so. If you draw an unsatisfactory shape, try to correct it before you erase it or you will tend to repeat the mistake. Draw any stalks or connecting lines first, then add the main shapes, bearing in mind the ways of varying the elements in the design listed in the last chapter. If you have difficulty in making it fit together harmoniously, try cutting out the shapes in a different coloured paper so that you can move them around to assess alternative ways of grouping them; or lay a sheet of tracing paper over the design to try an idea on it, which again can be moved. At this stage you are concerned only with the structure of the design, that is, the lines you will need to transfer to the cloth, or to an appliqué backing paper.

You need not necessarily draw with a pencil; you could use a thick wash brush, charcoal or pastel, or anything else that will make a mark on paper, from a piece of stick to a piece of cloth over your finger and dipped in paint. This will give you enormous variety of line and texture – you may accidentally discover some beautiful abstract shapes. It may be that they will suggest some theme to you such as flight, moving water, explosion, or energy. You might draw further shapes or research the subject for new ones in books. It is fun to experiment.

— Using a Photo

If you feel uninspired by the last two paragraphs you may be happier using photography, preferably your own, so that it is truly your source of inspiration. Otherwise you will find endless ideas in specialised photography of cell structures, and close-up photography. You will find plenty in your local library. Try the idea, mentioned in the last chapter, of searching in a photo with two L-shaped pieces of paper. If you are looking for something more formal you may find it in old textiles, Greek and Egyptian ornaments, peasant art. Take some motif from your source of inspiration and use it in your own way.

— Cut Paper Designing

A well tried and widely advocated method of designing is the use of cut paper. This is one of the best ways, so it is important to mention it. The advantage is that the pieces can be moved about until a balanced arrangement is achieved, whereas the drawn line or shape is static. When you are happy with your arrangement, you can take a tracing; with this method you can give yourself unlimited choice.

— A Library of Paper Shapes

It is a good idea to prepare yourself a little library of shapes, and keep them in plastic bags. Every time you see a new leaf or other interesting shape, record it. Draw it freely on the top layer of a large sheet of paper folded into four, as many times as you can fit it in the paper, varying the size and shape as much as possible. Cut shapes out through all four thicknesses, then you will have plenty to choose from. If you use greaseproof paper and place the pieces on a dark paper, you will get the value of overlapping shapes. Do this with as many leaf, petal and any other interesting shapes that you can find. With a good supply of these you need never be short of ideas; you will find that they can be combined to make new shapes and are self perpetuating.

— Collecting Inspiration

Collect also anything that appeals to you in the way of design: postcards, magazine cuttings, old calendars and greetings cards. It is surprising how much you will find if you start looking. They are something to fall back on when you need a new idea.

— Useful Books

If you have access to books old enough to be illustrated with etchings rather than photographs, you will find them a fruitful source of inspiration, particularly nature books. They are almost ready made machine embroidery designs, being entirely in line. The two crafts have a lot in common. Of today's books, the Dover publications are among the best; the firm produces all kinds of books to help the artist. It publishes one book in particular that every hand or machine embroideress should have. *Japanese Design Motifs* contains a wealth of small motifs of every kind that could be enlarged to the size of a curtain or be as small as a pincushion. You will find something in it that you can use for your starting point. The starting point is the most difficult part. Once that is established, most people can competently choose their colours, textures and stitches.

To develop creativity, it is a very good exercise to explore the possibilities of one design in depth by doing it several times in varying scales, colours, and techniques. Weeks can be spent on the design without repetition.

To sum up, short of taking your own photos or making sketches for inspiration, books and magazines are likely to be your mainstay. Be sure that you use authentic references rather than some cheap adaptations that might be used in advertisements.

— Experiments for Abstract Design

If you don't have time to sketch or take photographs, you may like to try some more experimental ideas, such as dropping ink onto paper and blowing it through a straw, or blotting it by pressing another paper onto it. Printing with leaves, garden objects, or a carved potato are very rewarding ways to create texture and border patterns.

— Choosing Your Own Method

How you like to design is a personal matter. Some people dislike fiddling about with paper and scissors, they prefer to work directly on to the cloth and this is certainly the best way for appliqué. You may find that starting in the middle of the hoop generates ideas. Other people prefer to have a design fully worked out before venturing onto the cloth. It doesn't matter how you set about it, but do occasionally take time to experiment, try new ideas and new combinations of stitching. Think about the ideas in this book and see how you can develop them further. Sometimes interesting things happen by accident. The skill is to exploit them when they do. Be flexible and adventurous with new ideas.

— Building the Design

Designing can be described as a building process. Whether you use cut paper or fabric shapes, you should start somewhere near the middle and work outwards considering the spaces as you go. It is easiest to work in an empty space rather than have to incorporate things already in that space; however, sometimes it is necessary to plan focal points first, such as round the neck of a garment, in which case you must build up the design between them.

— Things to Avoid

Whatever method of designing you choose, there are criteria for you to observe. To take an obvious example, in a free flowing design of flowers there should not be three flower centres in a dead straight line or two centres in line with the corner of the work. This brings in an inharmonious geometric element. A line or curves should not lead out of a design on one side only, because they will lead the eye outwards instead of allowing it to rest comfortably on the focal areas. It should be balanced by another one or two lines leading out elsewhere (but never exactly opposite). This seems like commonsense; it is, but there are many less obvious design weaknesses that creep in unnoticed. There is often one small part of a design that does not seem to be right; it may be that there are two shapes near each other which are too similar in size or character, or it may be that opposite edges of a shape are too parallel. You may need to compress existing shapes slightly to fit a new one in the awkward area or space them out to fill it. This is where cut paper shapes are so useful. Another way to tackle the problem is to trace the outlines of the design and then cut up and re-arrange them or at least try out alternatives on tracing paper placed over the work instead of on the work itself. But be watchful particularly for inadvertent straight lines in flowing designs.

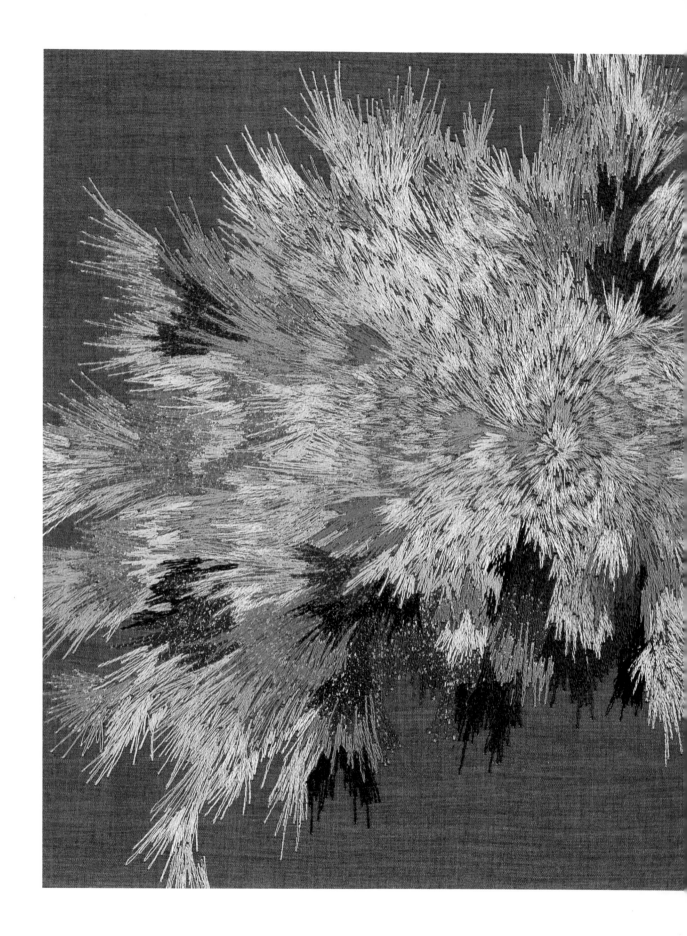

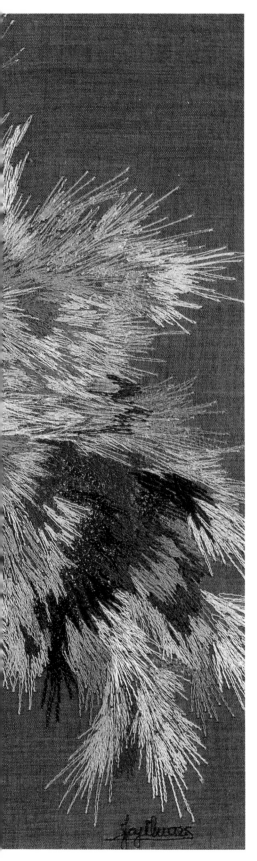

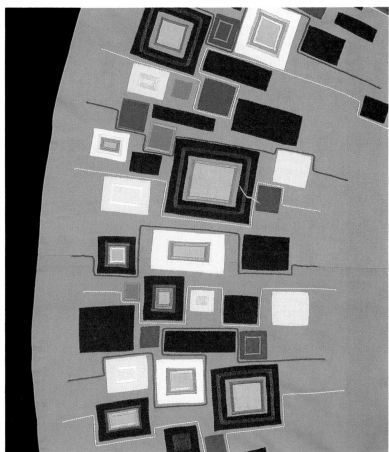

Appliqué skirt by Joy Clucas, using poly-cotton fabric with applied perle and soft embroidery cotton.

'A Touch of Frost' by Joy Clucas, 37.5×34.5cm (14¾× 13½in). Free straight stitching with loosened bobbin thread, which shows on the change of direction. Many sewing and machine embroidery cottons were used.

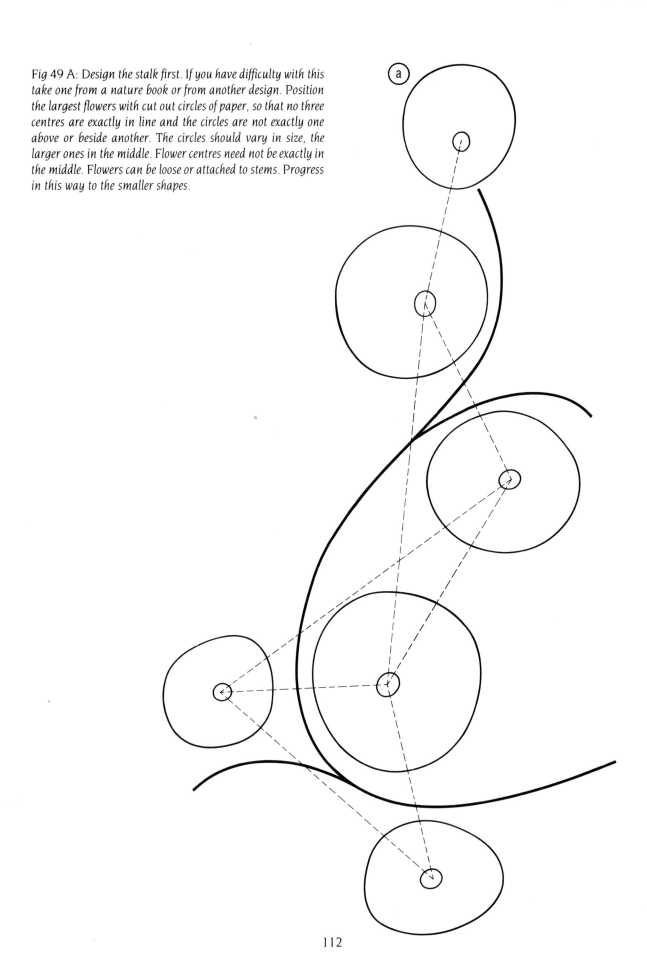

Fig 49 A: Design the stalk first. If you have difficulty with this take one from a nature book or from another design. Position the largest flowers with cut out circles of paper, so that no three centres are exactly in line and the circles are not exactly one above or beside another. The circles should vary in size, the larger ones in the middle. Flower centres need not be exactly in the middle. Flowers can be loose or attached to stems. Progress in this way to the smaller shapes.

a

Fig 50 B: The stalk of diagram 49 with a different flower arrangement. Notice that the side stalks are of different lengths and spacing.

Fig 51 C: Finally, work out details, making minor adjustment to stems if necessary. The dotted line shows a design fault that is corrected by moving the shape to the right, making a better arrangement of the lower three flowers.

'Ghosts at Dusk' by Alvena Hall of West Lakes, South Australia. This beautiful work is the fourth of a series of six works called 'Regeneration'. It was inspired by the bush fires of 1983 near Adelaide. It shows how painting, spraying and dying cloth can combine well with machine embroidery.

'Flotsam', 26.5×23cm (10½×9in), shows two techniques that one would never imagine putting together. It was a lucky accident seeing the two embroideries together; the top is free stitching on tulle in white and pale blue and the Elna disc 142 was used for the presser foot lines on salmon pink fabric.

— Adjustment of Design Weaknesses —

When you are working freely, designing as you go as in 'A Touch of Frost', you will find it hard to avoid the design faults just described. It is always necessary, after the main areas of the design are done, to go back over them to break any straight edge or badly shaped line or space. You may need to add emphasis or to make a demarcation between two colours that don't blend, or you may need to adjust the shape. It never matters how dense the stitching is to correct the clumsiness of the edge. Awareness of design and balance is something you will develop with practice. In the meantime, seek the critical eye of.anyone around you; they can often see things that you can't, you are too familiar with it. Also get someone else to check your trimming; it is surprising how often when you see a work after some time, the first thing to hit you is a linking thread that should have been cut off.

— Planning Colour —

If you are working with simple shapes and very few colours, it can be more expedient to plan one colour at a time. A good example of this is the blue appliqué skirt. It is an entirely random design. All the navy shapes were laid in position first until they were in a balanced arrangement. Then the white and

116

very pale shapes were planned; some of the centres were cut out to expose the background fabric, which was quicker and better than adding another layer (which would have meant stitching through three fabrics). More squares were placed inside them. The touches of sharp colour were the last to be positioned. Without them the work would be dull. Notice how softer touches of the sharp colours are used in the stitching.

— Machine Embroidery with Other Textile Arts

This whole book has been about machine embroidery, but it will not be complete without saying that there are few boundaries left in the textile world; many encroach into others. Machine and hand embroidery can be used together, softly machine textured backgrounds can give an extra dimension to the main motif. It could also be used with tie dye and batik. Beware, though, of overdoing it. The latter two crafts are very rich in themselves, it would be easy to mar their own textures with machining. Rather choose an understated one, even a failure, work into it in much the same way as the sample on the printed fabric, strengthening the structure that is already there and adding texture. It will also combine with felt and paper making, knitting and weaving. There are many new avenues to explore; perhaps your development of these techniques will contribute to a sequel to this book.

'Space Man' by Andrew Wilden, age 9, Bishop William Ward School, Colchester, 22.5cm (9in). *The free textural stitching on this embroidery proves that perfect technique is not always essential, or even desirable.*

117

Further Reading

Care of Textiles
The Care and Presentation of Textiles Karen Finch & Greta Putnam (Batsford, 1985)

Design for Embroidery
Creative Wall Hangings and Panels Audrey Babington (David & Charles, 1982)
Designing for Embroidery from Ancient and Primitive Sources Jan Messent (Studio Vista, 1976)
Design in Embroidery Kathleen Whyte (Batsford, 1969)
Embroidery and Animals Jan Messent (Batsford, 1984)
Embroidery and Architecture Jan Messent (Batsford, 1985)
Embroidery and Nature Jan Messent (Batsford, 1980)
Embroidery and Colour Constance Howard (Batsford, 1986)
Fabric Pictures Eugenie Alexander (Mills and Boon, 1959)
Inspiration for Embroidery Constance Howard (Batsford, 1985)
Introducing Design in Embroidery Betty Chicken (Batsford, 1971) Good for children
Japanese Design Motifs compiled by the Matsuya Piece-Goods Store (Dover, 1972) This book is probably the most useful of all design inspiration books.
Lettering for Embroidery Pat Russell (Batsford, 1971)
Making Needlecraft Landscapes Mary Carroll (David & Charles, 1986)

Machine Embroidery Techniques
Charted Needle Design, Counted Cross Stitch and Needlepoint on the Sewing Machine Theta Happ (Delmar Creative Publications, Oklahoma City, 1984)
Gutermann Thread Painting Liz Hubbard (Search Press, 1985)
Landscape in Embroidery Verina Warren (Batsford, 1986)
Machine Embroidery: Lace and See-Through Techniques Moira Mcneill (Batsford, 1985). A comprehensive guide to all methods.
Machine Embroidery: A Complete Guide Christine Risley (Studio Vista, 1973, 1980). Mainly useful for study of trade machines but good for design ideas.
Machine Embroidery Technique and Design Jennifer Gray (Batsford, 1973) Trade machine orientated but very good for ideas.
Machine Embroidery with Style dj Bennett (Madrona Publishers, Seattle, 1980)
Machine Stitches Anne Butler (Batsford, 1976)
Machine Stitchery Gay Swift (Batsford, 1974)
The Complete Book of Machine Embroidery Robbie and Tony Fanning (Chilton, 1980)
The Creative Sewing Machine Anne Colman (Batsford, 1979, 1981)
The Joy of Machine Embroidery Regina Bartley (Henry Regnery, Chicago, 1976) Good for ideas.

Machine Patchwork
Machine Patchwork Dorothy Osler (Batsford, 1980, 1983)

Machine Quilting
The Complete Book of Machine Quilting Robbie and Tony Fanning (Chilton, 1980)

Suppliers

UK

Beads
Ells and Farrier Ltd, 5 Princes St, London W1R 8PH

Bias Bars
Craft Publications Unit SC, 5 West Hill, Aspley Guise, Milton Keynes MK17 8DP

Bias Bars and Quilting Supplies
Quilt Room, 37–9 High Street, Dorking, Surrey RH4 1AR

Fabric Suppliers
George Weil and Sons Ltd, 63–5 Riding House Street, London W1P 7PP. Silks and cottons.
Limericks, Hamlet Court Rd, Westcliffe on Sea. Cotton sheeting 90in wide; white and colours.
S. Borovick, 16 Berwick Street, London W1. Theatre, films, television and embroidery specialist, stockists for twinkle and crystal nylon.

Machine Embroidery Suppliers
Beldale Crafts, 121 Raby Road, Hartlepool, Cleveland TS24 8DT. Machine embroidery threads and dissolving fabrics.
C. and F. Handicraft (Supplies) Ltd, 346 Stag Lane, Kingsbury, London NW9 9AG. They will supply the name of your nearest DMC stockist.
Franklins 13A/15 St Botolphs Street, Colchester CO2 7DU. Specialist needlecraft and knitting store, including DMC machine embroidery cotton. Mail order and callers.

Pauline Deverell 'Mylor', Church Hill, West End, Southampton, Hampshire SO5 5AT. Fabrics and threads, mail order.

Mary Allen, Wirksworth, Derbyshire DE4 4BN.

MacCulloch and Wallis Ltd, 25–26 Dering Street, London W1R 0BH. Vanishing muslin.

Nottingham Handicrafts Ltd, 17 Ludlow Hill Road, Melton Road, West Bridgford, Nottingham NG2 6HD.

Regent Sewing Machines, 13 & 15 Station Lane, Hornchurch, Essex RM12 6JL. Madeira thread.

Silken Strands, 33 Kinksway, Gatley, Cheadle, Cheshire SK8 4LA. Mail order only. Natesh and Madeira machine embroidery thread.

The Workbasket, 38 High Street, Great Missenden, Bucks. DMC machine embroidery and Madeira metallic threads.

Thread Bare, 5 Forester Drive, Fence, Burnley, Lancs BB12 9PG. Madeira thread.

USA

Dissolving paper (examination paper)

Surgical Supply Houses, Crescent City Surgical Supplies, Lime Street, Metairie, Louisiana. Large quantities only.

Machine Embroidery Suppliers

Aardvark Adventures, 1191 Bannock, Livermore, California 94550.

Bernina Sewing Centre of Hurst, 848 W. Pipeline Rd, Hurst Texas 76053.

Doris Carmack, 10841 La Batista Ave, Fountain Valley, California 92708.

Doris Neal, 53 Weibel Avenue, Saratoga Springs, NY 12866.

Patsy Leeper, 1805 Buddinbrook Lane, Winston-Salem NC 27106.

Patsy Kuppenbender, 10753 SE 29th Street, Milwaukie, OR 97222.

Sew Art International, PO Box 550 Bountiful, Utah 84010.

Sew Craft, Box 6146, South Bend, IN 46660.

Treadleart, 25834 Narbonne Avenue, Lomita, CA 90717.

Theta Happ, Theta's School of Sewing, 2508 NW 39th St, Oklahoma 73112.

Curved Elna Needle plate

Tecla, 120 E. Birch, Brea, California 92621.

For a comprehensive list of American stockists refer to *The Complete Book of Machine Embroidery* by Robbie and Tony Fanning.

AUSTRALIA

Beads

Artisan Craft Supplies, 502 Marmion St, Booragoon, WA 6154.

Lucas & Co, Upper Level, Queens Arcade, 77 Queen St, Brisbane, Qld 4000.

Maria George Pty Ltd, 179 Flinders Lane, Melbourne 3000.

Photios Bros Pty Ltd, 66 Druitt St, Sydney 3000.

Machine Embroidery Suppliers

Coats Modern Accessories, 64 Balmain St, Richmond, Vic. 3121.

Coats-Semco, 8A George St, Sandringham, Vic. 3191.

Cottage Crafts, 462 Fullarton Rd, Myrtle Bank, SA 5064.

Handcraft Supply Sales, 15 Bibby St, Chiswick, NSW 2064.

Hardies Handicrafts, 144 Adelaide St, Brisbane, Qld 4000.

Index

Numbers in *italics* refer to illustrations